YOU ARE BORING

BUT YOU ARE *UNIQUELY* BORING

25 Models for Writing Your Memoir

DEDICATION

For Tom and Ken

Contents

INTRODUCTION

LOUISE'S TURN

I don't know if you're boring or not. I do know that most people come to the task of writing memoir with some self-loathing and dread. To take the time to write of one's own experience—time that might be better spent planting iris or memorizing Civil War battles—seems to some wasteful, maybe even selfish. No matter. That's just your inner busybody critic, scrubbing your psyche with an abrasive soap to keep you behaving appropriately and not shaming your family, and yourself, by writing anything at all. You're not a writer, you silly Billy.

Ban that critic! Writing memoir is celebrating an essential life, with its diverse experiences, good, bad, and ugly and writing it with authenticity. Write it the way you remember it, quoting the important and secondary characters, describing the messes as well as the angle of sunlight on your bedspread in the morning. Describe what you ate, what you did for fun, how you spent your money, how your parents argued or never argued, how you were sick all of fifth grade, how your mother wanted you to be a brain surgeon. Describe the life you lived, not the one you wished you'd lived, (or you could write side-by-side entries: here's what happened; here's what I wish had happened).

Living, fretting, surviving, dreaming, falling over, and getting back up: it's all worth writing down. It's making your mark on the planet and being a witness: I was here, and it mattered.

Why memoir and not autobiography? The two terms are often blurred, but while autobiography is the story of a full life, memoir

1

is a more narrow form, describing important chunks of your life as the growing up years and stopping at high school graduation, or telling about a marriage, or the building of a successful career. Gore Vidal delineates between the two in his own memoir, *Palimpsest: A Memoir:* "A memoir is how one remembers one's own life, while an autobiography is history, requiring research, dates, facts double-checked." Both the memoir and the autobiography are assumed to be true, that is, the events really happened.

Writing from memory is as dodgy as memory itself, which can be filled with inaccuracies, misinterpretations, and emotional overtones. When you write about growing up in a large family, for example, your siblings may not remember events in the same way or with the same importance as you do. I know a large family where the members are not agreed on whether their father was an alcoholic or not. So, you need to claim your memoir as *your* truth, even if it doesn't match how others remember the same events.

Memoirist Patricia Hampl has a forgiving definition of writing memoir: "It's not about nailing down facts, but gathering impressions from the past." *Gathering impressions from the past:* we can all do that.

Off the top of your head, which impressions of the past are most immediate in your mind? Which memories are most compelling? Start with one of these and then find another. Jot topics down during the day as you remember them, and then choose one or two for your writing time each day. Don't worry about chronology and organization. That is a job for a later time.

Memoirs take all kinds of forms and shapes: there is the coming-of-age memoir, the revenge memoir, the survival memoir, abuse memoirs, war memoirs, celebrity memoirs, and many others. Even if you're not a celebrity, I can imagine writing a memoir called, "My Life as a Star." You may know at the outset the precise subject of your memoir, but you may not. It will assert itself as you write.

Who (dead or alive) doesn't want you to write a memoir? You might want to write that person an unsent letter (see page 103 and explain why you're writing your story, so you can get on with it.

ANN'S TURN

I love, love, love this sentence: "Off the top of your head, which impressions of the past are most immediate in your mind?" Here's my list:

- The smell of a grassy field at night after a football game has ended.
- The feel of my cat Clio's coat after she'd been sitting in the afternoon sun.
- The shame of feeling socially awkward in the seventh grade.
- The flood of hormonal joy after the birth of a baby.
- The realization that I was dying after the birth of our last child.
- The scent of pine filling the entryway whenever we first brought a Christmas tree into our house.
- The fear I felt when I wondered if my parents would ever get a divorce.
- The sense of awe that overcame me when I saw the ocean for the first time.

See? I dashed that off the top of my head in less than five minutes while listening to a boring speech. (Why are there so many boring speeches in life? I ask you!)

You know what I *can't* remember, though? My first real kiss.

Isn't that odd?

YOUR TURN

Now it's your turn to list five (or more) impressions of the past that are most immediate in your mind. Do it quickly. Get ready. Get set. Go!

See? That wasn't so hard, was it? You have a handful of things to write about, and we haven't even made it to the first chapter yet.

CHAPTER 1

Kick Out Your Inner Critic

LOUISE'S TURN

Writing is a creative act fraught with psychic tension. The blank computer screen shows the cursor beating like your pulse, waiting, waiting, waiting for the first sentence of your long awaited memoir. Will that sentence be intelligent, humorous, witty, wise, and wonderful? Will that sentence knock the breath out of your readers with its insight and literary elegance?

Not unless you're William Bloody Shakespeare.

Most likely, you'll begin with, "I was born on September 11, 1942 in Utrecht, the Netherlands to Lodewijk and Geertje Roos." Immediately, your inner critic will rise up and eviscerate you for writing such a common and mundane first sentence: *Can't you think of something more original? Should there be a comma after "Netherlands"? Are you even sure you spelled your father's name correctly? Geez. Hit the delete button before anybody sees what a lousy writer you are.*

Begin again: "I was born at home on Bernard de Waalstraat 21 in Nazi-occupied Utrecht, Holland." The inner critic won't be any happier with this new sentence: *Oh, now we're taking the Anne Frank approach! Nazi-occupied Holland? Isn't that emotionally manipulative, as if you were born into a clear and present danger? You weren't Jewish! And Holland is a province, not a country. What's your problem?*

You can spend hours writing first sentences or first paragraphs and hating yourself, or you can avoid the whole problem by deciding to write imperfectly. It's a first draft. You can make changes later. A first draft is a spilling out of first thoughts without regard to form, punctuation, grammar, and spelling. It's just getting it down. The best way to do this is to write fast, so fast that the inner critic can't interrupt your thoughts.

Let me share a technique used by many professional writers called "rush writing" that addresses the anxieties of writing. It's a *timed* writing, and this is how you do it:

- Set a timer (cell phone or oven timer will do nicely) for a short time, five or ten minutes, and write the first page of your memoir.

- Write as fast as you can, focusing on the beginning of your life. If you lose your train of thought, don't stop. Simply write in your confusion: *I forgot what I was writing about—I can't think.* The main rule is to keep writing no matter what. Sometimes, you find the subject again or you may go off on a tangent unrelated to what you've begun. Tangents can be more interesting than the original idea. It doesn't matter. Write fast. Write from your subconscious.

- Don't worry about spelling and grammar. Don't worry about syntax. Write until the timer buzzes, then finish your sentence and stop. In ten minutes, you'll write more than a page. Maybe, it's all nonsense. Usually, there's a sentence or a phrase that carries energy and truth. Maybe that will be your first sentence.

- Give your writer's cramp a break and then repeat the whole process. Write again about your beginnings and don't allow yourself to repeat anything you wrote the first round. Do this until you can't think of any new way to state your beginnings.

The advantage of writing fast, of writing your first thoughts, is that it allows you to record your thoughts before you can censor them. It separates the writer (creator) in you from the destructive critic. Our critics encourage the myth that writing is a high and lofty endeavor, and unless we can do it like Virginia Woolf or Vladimir Nabokov, we ought not to try. That's foolishness. Certainly, you can write about your own life, which is an inexhaustible subject, and no one knows more about that subject than you. Unlike critical writing, you can write authoritatively, without proof or footnotes. Your life is the proof. No one can argue with your experience, with your unique view of the world. It's the critic in us who tells us we can't write. Kick the critic. Write imperfectly. Write fast.

ANN'S TURN

Ugh. My inner critic has been working overtime lately, and he/she/it is driving me crazy. So I'm going to take Louise's advice and kick out him/her/it. Watch me!

ME: Hey, you there!
INNER CRITIC: Are you talking to me?
ME: Yes.
INNER CRITIC: (sounding impressed and even a little intimidated by my commanding tone): Why?
ME: Because I'm kicking you out! That's why.

Okay. Wow. Yes. I feel better now.

YOUR TURN

Take one of those impressions of the past you jotted down at the end of "The Introduction" and do a rush write, using that impression as your topic. Follow Louise's suggestions:

1. Set a timer for five or ten minutes.
2. Write as fast as you can.
3. Don't stop. Keep your hand moving the entire time.
4. Don't worry about spelling or grammar or syntax.
5. Stop when the buzzer rings.

Following this process *every day* helps you stare down your inner critic. And following this process every day helps you stare down your inner critic every day. Many professional writers write first drafts fast. You should too.

Here's something else you can do while you're at it. Give your inner critic a name. Create an annoying persona around that name, and then dismiss that person whenever he/she starts barking in your ear. For example, if your inner critic (let's call her Gladys) begins telling you that you can't write, all you have to do is roll your eyes and say, "There goes Gladys again, just yakkity-yak-yakking. Pipe down, Gladys!"

Bottom line? You can do this!

CHAPTER 2

You Were Born

LOUISE'S TURN

Your story doesn't begin with your first memory; it begins before memory. You'll have to quote others. My father said I was born with my eyes wide open, and that I kept them open the rest of the afternoon, "looking at everything."

My mother said I would not nurse, so they fed me with a silver spoon. Perhaps they exaggerated. I was their first child and what must have seemed like the brightest star in the sky at the time.

Did they even own a silver spoon? Or did she mean a silver-colored spoon? A metal spoon with a silver hue? I used to like the idea of an opulent beginning with that sterling silver spoon in my mouth. Then I think of my parents: an earnest electrician from Utrecht and his wholesome peasant bride from Breukelen. Probably not sterling silver.

They wanted me. The two of them were so excited, they put up a bassinet with lace curtains months before I was born. My father bought a Teddy bear.

I was born at home in my parents' bed after twenty-four hours of labor. It was September 11, 1942, a Friday afternoon, 3:15 p.m. Home was a three-story brick townhouse at Bernard de Waalstraat

21, Zuilen, Utrecht, the Netherlands. I weighed about seven-and-a-half pounds.

American friends used to ask me, "Why were you born in the Netherlands?" as if my parents had wandered off the North American grid, aimlessly, and had their baby in a foreign country. Were they on vacation? Were they in the diplomatic corps? Was my father working for an American company in the Netherlands?

No, they were born-and-bred Dutch, and they came from a long line of more born-and-bred-Dutch ancestors. People with names like deWith, Copier, Roos, Bijleveld, Verkerk, Giese, VanRinsum and Van der Verguldenbijl. I am so Dutch. I was named after my father, Louis, (pronounced like the French Louie) and my mother's sister, Marie, who was known as Riet, for short. Tante Riet.

More than two years before I was born, the Nazis occupied the Netherlands. I was born in a war zone.

ANN'S TURN

Seriously, the only thing anybody—my parents, my grandparents, a few aunts and uncles—seem to remember about me is that I stuck my tongue out at people when I was first born.

So charming!

Here's the deal. I'm convinced this wasn't an act of infant defiance. It was me just trying to get coordinated. To this day whenever I do something physical my tongue kind of hangs out of the side of my mouth. You know. Like a dog.

Also charming!

This is an Edwards thing. I blame my father. And I've passed this trait along. The other day when my four-year-old granddaughter was coloring, I noticed that her tongue was hanging out of the side of her mouth.

So she can blame me.

Cue the music. It's the circle of life.

YOUR TURN

Got it? Now write a list of your own firsts. Choose one from the list and write about it. Then write another. And another. It's addictive, isn't it?

CHAPTER 3

The First Memory

LOUISE'S TURN

When was that first moment when you arose out of the cottoned cocoon of babyhood and experienced your first conscious memory? Some people remember events as early as age one. For others, it comes much later. What image was so beautiful or scary that it has remained with you forever? Here's mine:

My mother sews me a lamb costume out of white flannel. I am three years old and have a part in the church Christmas program. I stand at the edge of the table where she works looking up as she pushes the flannel under the needle with one hand and turns the handle of the sewing machine with the other. I am elated that this will be my costume. It is my first awareness of anticipation.

This is my second first memory: I am wearing the lamb costume onstage. I have one line, which Mother has rehearsed with me. When it is my turn, I speak in a loud, confident voice, and the audience breaks into laughter. I am surprised, but I like the reaction. I like making people laugh. I will like it for the rest of my life.

I call this my second first memory, because it is closely related to the first memory but doesn't occur on the same day. I have other first memories: memories so early, that I cannot place them chronologically. Mostly they are images: my maternal grandmother

(Opoe) pulling me into her apron when I am the first to get up in the morning and find her in her kitchen. My maternal grandfather (Opa) doesn't close his eyes when the rest of the family says the blessing on the food. "Opa didn't close his eyes," I say.

"How do you know?" he asks, a faint smirk on his lips.

Opoe sits on the floor with my brother, Gerard, and me in her lap, and she claps her hands and sings this clapping song:

Klap es in je handjes, blij blij blij
Op je boze bolletjes, allebei.
Zo varen de scheepjes voorbij!

I remember riding on the back of my father's bike to get to church in Utrecht. I remember spending Sunday afternoons with my father's parents: Opa would read Gerard and me the funny papers, pointing at each cartoon as he read. He gave us the gold bands from his cigars that we wore around our fingers. Oma made chocolate pudding. At Christmas she gave us marzipan shaped as fruit.

Sometimes when students write their first memories, they get nervous and defensive: "I don't remember anything before kindergarten or middle school." It doesn't matter when you had the first memory, it matters what your first memory was.

ANN'S TURN

For a long time if you'd asked me what my first memory is, I would have said this: the day they brought my brother John home from the hospital. I was the oldest and the only, and although I didn't realize it at the time, that is a sweet, sweet family spot to occupy. So what if my first-time mother, herself an only child, was so afraid of accidentally giving me germs that she wore a surgical mask around me for the first few months of my life! I was adored. By her. By my father. By her parents. (I'm sure my father's parents liked the idea of me just fine, but since they had fourteen children of their own and a boatload of grandkids by the time I rolled around, another baby in the family was pretty much yesterday's news.)

Anyway.

One day my mother went away. And then she brought back something all wrapped up like a Sunday roast. Except the roast wasn't wrapped up in white butcher paper. No. It was swaddled in a blue blanket.

My parents had a son.

I watched in dismay as they unwrapped him, spread the blue blanket on a chair, and propped up that red, skinny, barely sentient being in the center of said chair and started taking pictures of it.

What?!

My maternal grandparents were also there. So were a clutch of great-aunts and one great-uncle named Bob who had a large nose and smoked a pipe. These were people who were normally fascinated by my little dances and squeaky two year-old voice, but now? I was just another B-lister trying to worm my way into the disco while the bouncer and everybody stood aside for the shiny new A-lister, aka "my brother."

I know. I was young—so young that people have a hard time believing I can remember that day in such sharp detail. But please believe me when I say I do.

To continue—when I realized all eyes were on my brother, who shall be known henceforth as "the interloper," I decided to take matters into my own hands. I would run away! And thereby cause everyone to come look for me! So, accompanied by the family boxer, I slipped outside and stood beneath the crabapple tree, waiting for people to come find me.

How long did I stand under the tree?

Probably only five minutes. But it felt like five years. Five hundred years.

Clearly I need to recalculate my running-away-plan.

So then I decided to hide with the dog in our basement. Surely the parents and grandparents and great aunts and pipe-smoking great uncle would organize a search party and look for me in the basement.

But they didn't.

How long did I hide in the basement? Would you believe me if I told you I'm still here? Yes. It's true. I've grown old in this basement—stooped and gray-haired and covered with cobwebs, waiting for my parents to stop looking at my baby brother on the blanket and come looking for me. I'm the Miss Haversham of Basements, except without the wedding dress part. Obviously, I never had the chance to get a wedding dress because I've been here in the basement (thanks to my parents) ever since that fateful day when I turned two-and-a-half . . .

Except now that I think about it, I have an even earlier memory. My mother was hugely pregnant with John when she took me to ride the Ferris wheel at Liberty Park in Salt Lake City. I adored everything about the ride. When we reached the top, I felt like a bird, roosting in the tree limbs. Or a fairy. Yes, I was a fairy waving my magic wand, doing spells and other fairy-type things!

And so I was both surprised and outraged when my mother said to the attendant as we reached the bottom after only one complete rotation that her little girl was afraid and could we please get off now.

Afraid?

Excuse me, but afraid?!

I realized right then that I was being used as an excuse, because my mother was the one who didn't like heights. I deeply resented this, although later on I realized that one of the advantages of having kids in this life is that you can use them as an excuse whenever you need to.

I'm sorry. I can't go tonight because my kids are sick.

I'm sorry. I have to stay home to help my kids with their homework.

I'm sorry. You'll have to stop the Ferris wheel because my daughter is afraid.

Yes. Kids are awesome that way. And if you give them enough years, siblings can sometimes turn out to be okay, too.

YOUR TURN

Write your earliest memory and then write another. Try this: set the timer for five minutes and begin each sentence with "I remember." Dig as far back as you can. Write fast. Don't think; don't plan. Let it rise up from inside of you. Have faith in the process. I remember. I remember.

CHAPTER 4

Other Important Firsts

LOUISE'S TURN

There are other firsts you'll want to write about, and only you can choose which are meaningful to you. Some examples: the first time you owned a car—it ate up alternators like doughnuts, the first date, the first kiss—crooked, the first time you rode a bicycle, the first time you wore high heels and fell into the pyracantha bush in your prom dress. The first time you realized how babies were made. The first time you traveled alone as an adult:

I was twenty-three and flew to Paris two days before meeting my young husband in Bonn, Germany. I knew no French. The only preparation I had made was to ask my friend, Dennis Garff, who had lived in Paris, to suggest a clean but inexpensive hotel where the staff spoke English.

He had just the place, a small family-owned hotel within spitting distance of the Eiffel Tower. I wouldn't need a reservation, he said. I printed the name and address on a card and placed it in my purse.

Flying into Orly Airport on a sunny morning, the red tiled roofs rising to greet me, was an exhilarating moment. Paris was an architectural wonderland. It was the setting for an Audrey Hepburn movie, and I, for a brief moment, was Audrey Hepburn.

Once in a cab, I produced the card with the neatly printed address of the hotel and showed it to the driver. He nodded and we were off. I sat back in my seat confident in my ability to traverse Paris without a glitch.

Soon I stood in front of a hotel counter with a polite looking concierge in a dark suit behind it. I smiled and told him in English that I wanted a room for two nights. He lifted his shoulders in a sympathetic gesture, spread his hands, one of them passing over the registrar, and spoke in French. French! And though I didn't speak a word of French, I knew in a nanosecond that 1) he spoke no English, 2) the hotel was full, and 3) I had no idea of where to go or what to do.

The anxiety rose up in me to become full terror. I couldn't breathe. My mouth gaped open, preparing to wail out my anguish: I am alone in Paris with very little money, and I'll be thrown out in the street and will have to prostitute myself to live, and I'll never see my family again. Waaaaah!

The concierge, like a well-trained doctor, reached across the counter and held my arm tightly as if to steady me. He waved his other arm and shook his head. No, no, no. Did he say that? Holding my arm, he moved around the counter, picked up my suitcase, and pulled me out the door, down the street, and into another hotel. He spoke to the new concierge in French, set down my suitcase, smiled at me, and pointed to the counter as if to say, "This is your new home." Then he disappeared.

The new concierge said, "You want to stay for two nights?" in English, beautiful English. Yes, I did. Yes. Thank you. I signed in and was taken to my room which was the size of a prison cell but more pleasant. Thank you, Universe.

Did I go out and see Paris?

Not that first day. I stayed in bed under the covers to pull myself together. The next day I went out, walked about, spent the afternoon in the Louvre. I didn't eat for two days.

When it was time to take a cab to the train station, I said, "Train station."

The cabbie shrugged his shoulders, lifted his arms, hands pointed outward, palms up, which clearly meant, "I have no idea what you're talking about."

So I did an imitation of a train making chuffing noises, rotating my arms like wheels. He understood. Did I want to go North or South? I understood that much.

I didn't know. He took a guess and took me to the North Station, which was an excellent guess, and I found the train to Bonn, Germany, where they spoke German, which I'd studied in college, and where my husband waited for me.

ANN'S TURN

I think this particular topic (thanks, Louise!) calls for one of my lists.

- **First time I saw the ocean:** I was nine years old. My parents pulled over to the side of the road in Somewhere Southern California. Johnny and I stripped to our underwear in the back of the family station wagon and ran shrieking down the sandy hillside so we could dive headfirst into a wall of glittering waves.

- **First pet:** a dog. A wonderful fawn female boxer named Princess—Priny for short. She was my best friend. I can still remember how warm her coat felt against the palm of my hand on a summer's day.

- **First plane ride:** I was, to paraphrase Stevie Nicks, on the edge of sixteen. I flew to Hawaii with my mother and father, who had just been made head coach at BYU, which meant he got to take the glam recruiting trips now. I threw up on that first flight—either from motion sickness or nerves. Who can say?

- **First kiss:** Timmy Anderson kissed me in my basement behind our couch. We were both six.

- **First proper kiss:** Gah. This is so weird, but I don't remember. What does this say about me?

- **First time I noticed my husband:** He was wearing a torn sweatshirt working on a bicycle at the end of a dark hallway channeling James Dean. Of course I was interested!

- **First time I gave birth:** I said, "Wow! That hurt more than I thought it would."

YOUR TURN

By now you're getting a sense for how this book works. Louise and Ann throw a topic out there and write about it, thus creating a model for you. You'll notice that their pieces aren't very long, and that's just fine. Remember that a series of small essays can grow into a larger and very satisfying collection.

It's your turn now. Write about another first, and another.

CHAPTER 5

How Did You Become You?

LOUISE'S TURN

Long before I was a writer, I was a reader. I can still see the floor to ceiling loaded bookcases in the Hamilton School library cared for with devotion by the venerated spinster, Miss Rollo, the librarian. The books were organized into sections: girls' books, boys' books, animal books, picture books, non-fiction, and so on. They were clearly demarcated from each other. Once I discovered the girls' books, I never deviated from them. The first novel I remember reading was *Ellen Tibbits* by Beverly Cleary.

Our classroom visited the library twice a week for an hour. Miss Rollo sometimes asked us to report on the book we were reading at the beginning of class, so that class members could get ideas for their next read. I raised my hand and gushed about *Ellen Tibbits,* dramatizing the scene where Ellen's tights fall off in dance class while her nemesis, Otis, is watching. A scandalous scene for third graders! I held the book up for all to see.

The following library visit, I walked straight to *Ellen Tibbits* in the girls' section and was horrified to find that it was gone. I wasn't finished with it. Where was it? I wandered around the tables and found a group of boys leafing through its pages eagerly searching for the subversive falling tights scene. Miss Rollo took it from them and handed it to me. "You can read it when Louise is finished," she said to the boys.

I read a whole series of Penny Parish books by Janet Lambert. Penny lived in an army family. Her antagonist was the dark haired beauty, Louise. Don't think I didn't like reading my own name in print, especially when she was the "bad girl." The series began when the girls were young, but like *Anne of Green Gables* it took us well into their adult lives. Penny grew up to be an actress and married a cynical director who would not salute the flag! Such tension.

The summer after fourth grade, I read *Nancy Drew* non-stop.

Then I moved onto *Little Women* by Louisa May Alcott, where I thought I was unquestionably exactly like Jo March. In fact, I did turn out to be Jo March, who married a German professor, had four sons and grew up to write "girl books." I read *An Old Fashioned Girl*, also by Alcott, but when Miss Rollo suggested I diversify and read *Little Men*, which sat on the shelf marked "boys' books," I balked. No way did I want to read a book about boys. Disgusting.

Fortunately, Miss Rollo read *Charlotte's Web* aloud to us the year it was published. I loved it even though it was an "animal book." And fortunately too, my sixth grade teacher, Mr. Peterson, the color-blind art teacher, spent the last hour of every day reading us *Tom Sawyer* and *Huckleberry Finn* with a convincing southern accent. Good teachers go to heaven.

In junior high, I moved onto adult novels: *Gone With the Wind* and historical novels by Thomas B. Costain (*The Tontine*) and Lloyd C. Douglas (*The Robe* and *Magnificent Obsession*), and of course Hemingway's *A Farewell to Arms*.

In high school we were force-fed *Silas Marner* and *The Scarlett Letter*, neither of which I appreciated until I reread them much later. Mr. Iverson assigned Dickens's *David Copperfield*, in senior year. I was besotted with those characters and still quote them. Mrs. Gummidge: "I feel it more than others," and the carriage driver: "Barkus is willing." I've reread *David Copperfield* many times.

I also had a short lurid book habit in high school. I was old enough to buy my own paperbacks. The one I remember specifically was called *Chocolates for Breakfast*. The thing is, my mother read everything I read. Everything. She read these same nasty books and never commented. Finally, I realized that reading titillating fiction felt creepy, and besides I didn't want my mother reading it.

Mother was wise about this. If she had restricted my reading, I would have gone into defiance mode. Instead, she avoided a power struggle, and let me figure out for myself what was valuable reading and what was not. I came to my senses on my own.

And finally, the book that most changed my life was Salinger's, *The Catcher in the Rye*. Holden Caulfield's subversive voice took my breath away. You can write like that? I didn't know you could write with that kind of voice—a voice that is certainly the precursor of the contemporary young adult novel. I would copy that voice for years to come.

The reading habit continues in adulthood, and I've never met a librarian I didn't like, but none so beloved as the devoted Miss Rollo.

ANN'S TURN

Sometimes people ask me when I first began to write. And I tell them that I began writing even before I knew how to write.

My first stories were visual—pictures of a mouse family with matchbox beds and spools of thread for tables. My first stories were also oral—and not always true. I remember telling the kids at pre-school during show-(off)-and-tell-(lies) that a helicopter had landed in our yard the day before and that the pilot had handed me a new doll.

The kids were impressed. Of course they were, because HELICOPTER! But the teacher, while not confronting me directly, shot me looks of displeasure—which I thought was very rude of her. Who was she to get in the way of an awesome helicopter story?

Once I had words, I began to write my stories down—stories that tended to look a lot like whatever I happened to be reading at the time. For instance, I wrote many stories about a family of four Victorian sisters—one of whom was a tomboy who wanted to be a writer when she grew up. Her name was Scarlett and she looked a lot like me except she had green eyes, which is what you get when *Little Women* marries *Gone With the Wind* and they have a baby together.

I also wrote an entire novel the summer between my 8th and 9th grade years. It was a spy and romance caper—not unlike the kinds Phyllis Whitney used to write. The heroine looked a lot like me and the boy looked a lot like Mark Bowen, my neighbor on whom I had had a crush ever since the sixth grade.

I didn't write much in high school. I didn't read much either—except for the books I was assigned to read in English classes. (I have a theory by the way that you are not really yourself in high school. All that energy you used to have for books and ballet and all the interests you used to have go instead, to figuring out where you fit on the social food chain). However, by the time I hit college—and especially graduate school—I was at it again. I wrote a little bit of everything: fiction, poetry, reviews.

But what I discovered I enjoyed the most was writing little essays about my life.

And I've been doing that ever since.

YOUR TURN

Are you a soldier? Tinker? Tailor? Spy? Choose the vocation or avocation that best describes you and write how you became that version of you. It's worth noting that this topic alone—"My Early Life as a (fill in the blank)"—can generate a dozen (or more!) essays for one person. None of us is just one thing. Write about all the people you are.

CHAPTER 6

Life's Turning Points

ANN'S TURN

Before the accident I was always in motion. My mother remembers walking into the living room and seeing me, her 18-month old daughter, standing on the fireplace mantel. Why had I climbed all the way up there?

Oh, I don't know. It was there. And I hate this perpetual wind inside of me that made it soooooo uncomfortable for me to sit still. And focus.

Clearly, if I were a kid today, I'd be medicated. But in those days, short of putting them in a straight jacket, you just let kids like me crawl on top of things like fireplace mantels.

And then.

The accident.

Here's how it went down. When I was six years old I was riding bikes with my new husband, Timmy Anderson. We got married in my basement, and then we went for a bike ride in the church parking lot, where I hit a patch of gravel and completely wiped out, losing my dignity and some teeth in the process. My mother (always the good news!) cleaned me up, of course, but one of the scrapes became infected. The infection went systemic and attacked my kidneys. I landed in the hospital where I almost cashed in my chips, which would have been sad, because I was only six, and I didn't have that many chips yet. Then I spent another seven months in bed, being home-schooled by a district teacher who taught me how to read. And write. And because all that crazy random wind had been knocked out of me, I learned. I grew up to be a reader and a writer, all because of that bike accident.

One of the ways to write memoir is to think about your life in terms of its turning points. Sometimes we realize we're at a crossroads while we're there. Other times that moment becomes clearer in retrospect. But we all have turning points. Moves. New friendships. Failed romances. Births. Deaths. Accidents. Illnesses. Saying goodbye to an old church and joining a new church. Shedding an addiction. Making this turn instead of that one.

LOUISE'S TURN

In sixth grade, I was my best self: confident, funny, athletic. I was an artist and a writer. My drawings were showcased in the classroom and out in the hall. When Mr. Peterson had us each write a story, I was the only one who got to read hers aloud. What was so satisfying was that the class laughed in all the right places.

Sixth grade was my Mt. Olympus.

It all crashed down the summer between sixth and seventh grade. That summer I began calling my favorite teacher, Mr. Garrison, who I had in 6th and 7th grade, on the phone. I asked in a whispery voice, "Is John there?"

"John who?" he bellowed back. I'd break into nervous giggles and hang up. I don't want to think how often I might have called him that summer.

On the first day of seventh grade, Mr. Garrison gave a small and wry lecture on phone manners, his eyes locking with mine. I giggled all the way through it.

Later in the term, he approached me and said, "What's happened to you this year?"

I had no idea what he was talking about. "Nothing," I said.

"Why are you getting a C in health class?"

"I'm getting a C?" It wasn't possible. I didn't get C's.

"You missed a lot of assignments," he said.

"I did?" I was flummoxed. I thought I was the same girl I'd been in sixth grade, but now I was getting a C and hadn't been aware of the change. I thought I'd handed in all of my assignments, and I said so.

Mr. Garrison showed me his grade book with the blanks next to my name.

My mouth formed a surprised "O" at the sight of this evidence.

"You can do better," he said. "You're not paying attention."

I nodded my head and repeated his words to myself: I wasn't paying attention. I *had* paid attention, but now I wasn't.

I didn't know it then, but I recognized it later. I had gone through puberty. Nasty, mind-blowing puberty. It changed everything. And I didn't come out of it until I was sixty-five.

YOUR TURN

You already know what to do here, right? Make a list of turning points. Pick one. Write about it. And if you feel like it, do it again. List. Pick. Write. Repeat. You could fill an entire book with stories about important turning points.

CHAPTER 7

Memoir Mapping

LOUISE'S TURN

When describing a place or setting is inadequate, try drawing a map and then writing about it. Just as the act of writing will nudge lost memories to the foreground, drawing a map will also stimulate memory.

For example, who sat where around the kitchen table at dinnertime, and what took place there? Include the map in the memoir; it creates visual interest on the page.

In my family the map of the kitchen table looked like *diagram 1* (next page).

It's been fifty years since I lived at home, and what I first notice when I see what I've drawn is that even though my brother, Ted, is now 66 years old, I still call him by his boyhood name, Teddy. And my father is Daddy. Mother was always Mother.

Our table, which was chrome and plastic with chrome and yellow vinyl chairs, seated eight people. We only had six matching chairs, and so lesser chairs were brought in from other rooms. The two youngest children sat on chrome and vinyl stools at the corners. It was a chrome and vinyl world in the fifties. I see people now collecting mid-century furniture, calling it "vintage," and I want to throw up.

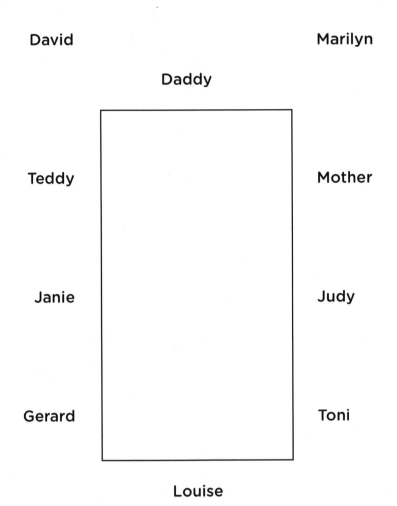

David   Marilyn

Daddy

Teddy   Mother

Janie   Judy

Gerard   Toni

Louise

Diagram 1

My favorite story around this table happened when Teddy was about four and sat at the corner stool long before David and Marilyn were ever dreamed of. My father, using his *Old Testament* voice, said that he needed to speak to us. Someone, he announced, had stolen money from Mother's wallet. He wanted to know who it was.

We children stared at him in complete innocence. In fact, I was innocent. Mother kept track of money like it was worth something, which in 1953, it was. The average house cost under $10,000 and gas cost 20 cents a gallon. So if a few quarters went missing, she would have noticed.

Who did it? My father wanted to know. He would not punish us, but he needed to know—*does any child believe this?* He looked into each face. Nothing.

"Then I'm going to have to give you the white flour test," he said. He instructed Gerard to get the large red canister of flour out of the hall closet. Daddy removed the lid and said, "Now, I'm going to pass this around the table. I want you each to dip your fingers into the flour. If you didn't take the money, your fingers will be white like the flour, but if you did take the money, the flour and your fingers will turn black as coal."

Even though I was eleven, I thought my father might actually have this kind of hocus pocus power. I wasn't sure. Judy would have been a baby, so he would have started with Toni, who dipped her fingers in and smiled a relieved smile when they came up white. I did the same. Whew. Then it was Gerard's turn. He hesitated as if this were a trap made especially for him, but then dipped in his fingers. White. Janie dipped in her fingers with confidence. Now the red canister sat squarely in front of Teddy, who was not dipping in his fingers.

"Go ahead," my father said.

Teddy slumped and swallowed hard.

My father nudged him. Teddy's lips puckered and skewered until a wail of guilt burst from his mouth. Anguished, loud howling filled the kitchen. My father picked him out of his chair and carried him into the bedroom, where they had "a talk." I have no idea what he said to him. Surely, he said something about telling the truth and not stealing—blah blah blah. It is worth it to be an honest child just so you don't have to hear these adult lectures.

I doubt anyone stole from my mother's purse again.

One last kitchen table story: Toni sat to my right. She was a finicky eater, and sometimes she simply didn't want to eat what Mother was serving. She would give me a sign, blinking eyes, nodding her head and shoving her plate closer to mine. I then, surreptitiously, stabbed the inedible item with my fork and slid it to my plate. It was an advantageous arrangement for both of us. I always wanted more, especially liver and onions, whereas Toni would rather eat a live toad than eat a piece of liver.

One Sunday afternoon, I thought she made the sign: eyes blinking, face aquiver, her plate inching closer to mine. I slid the roast beef onto my plate and ate it with voracious pleasure. Then the unthinkable happened. Toni cried out *magna voice*, "Who took my meat?"

"Whaaaat?" I cried. "I thought you made the sign!"

"What sign?" she asked, as if she'd never heard of this arrangement.

"You blinked your eyes; you moved the plate."

"I did not!" She turned to my father. "She ate my meat."

My father's *Old Testament* voice boomed, "What's going on?"

"She ate my roast beef. I like roast beef!"

"I thought—I thought she wanted me to eat it." Lame.

"You ate her meat?" There was no good answer to this question.

It was my turn for the adult lecture, which probably told me to stop eating my sister's meat and grow up! It tasted really good, though, and there wasn't another piece left.

Ideas for maps: the house where you grew up, or just the bedroom you shared with your sister. Draw a map of your neighborhood, labeling who lived in which house. Show the short cuts and the best places to hide for hide 'n seek. Point out whose garage roof you used to sit on, and where the ditch of water ran in front of your house.

Draw a map. Use colored pencils. Draw a scary face. Have fun with this.

ANN'S TURN

I took Louise's encouragement to have some fun with mapping and drew this seating chart from my 11th grade geometry class.

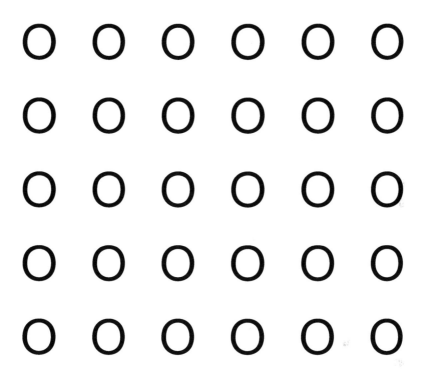

Diagram 2

I'm not sure it's accurate. Were there only 30 desks in that classroom?

I can't remember.

What I do remember are the boys who sat by me—Ken Schmidt, who loved Grand Funk Railroad so much he used to drum riffs of their album tracks on his desktop with a set of pencils; Czar Rudy, who had the coolest name in the history of the universe (because seriously—who was naming their babies "Czar" in the

1950's?); and Evan Perry, who was my 11th-grade boyfriend and an accomplished kisser.

OK, I was just a mess in that class. I didn't learn a thing, because I only had eyes for those boys and never paid a sweet lick of attention to our poor teacher, who occasionally smacked his yardstick across his desk—and mine—in an effort to get my attention.

It didn't work.

Nothing worked.

Nothing would have worked.

And as a result I learned a very important non-math lesson that later helped me as both a teacher and a mother. Once teenagers start showing up for each other, there's virtually nothing an adult (even an adult with a yardstick) can do to break up that dynamic.

YOUR TURN

You've probably already drawn up a map by now. Now write down a memory associated with your map.

At this point you may be saying to yourself, "Wow. This is so much easier than I thought it would be." You may also be thinking that anything this easy can't be the real thing, i.e. a memoir-in-the-making. Well, never fear. It is. It may be worth noting here that just as short pieces are easier to write, they're also easier to read. Your intended audience—children, grandchildren, friends—will thank you for that.

CHAPTER 8

The Best Day of Your Life

LOUISE'S TURN

All my fantasies, hopes and dreams came together in one splendid afternoon in New York City when I first visited the Sheldon Fogelman Literary Agency. I had talked to Sheldon Fogelman twice. The first time I called him on the advice of a writer, Richard Peck, whom Ann and I had taken to dinner when he was in Salt Lake (another best day).

I called him without thinking about what I was going to say and I ended up sounding like a doofus. I managed to tell him my name and that Richard Peck had told me to call him, but after that I fell into babbling and memory loss. I couldn't remember the names of any awards I had won on my two previous novels or even the names of the novels. I couldn't remember the name of my new manuscript, *The Unlikely Romance of Kate Bjorkman*. I sounded insane.

He said, "What is the age of your protagonist?"

I knew this one. "A seventeen-year-old girl."

"You should write about fourteen-year olds. There's a larger market for fourteen-year old protagonists."

"Yeah?"

"There's a real need for books for boys," he said. *Of course.* Then he asked, "Where do you live?"

I said, "Provo, Utah."

I heard a polite contempt in his hesitation. He said, "I like my writers to live in New York City."

Well, I thought, I'd like to live in New York City too, but I have this other life apart from writing and it's here in Provo, Utah. Like it or not.

I didn't say any of this.

He wanted to hang up on me, and who could blame him? How could I possibly be a decent writer when I couldn't talk with words?

But he left me an opening, a way to save myself: "Why don't you send me your manuscript, and I'll have a look at it."

"Okay, I will." We said good-bye.

He was rid of me.

By then, I did have faith in myself as a writer if not as an extemporaneous speaker, and I knew I had a terrific novel to sell. I also knew I would need to write a charming note to redeem my wordless self. If I were an accountant, I would have a copy of that note in my files, and would place it here word for word, but I am a scattered, artistic type ("kinda diffurnt," as my mother-in-law used to say about people like me) and I move to a new house every three years, so I have no idea where that letter is.

I do remember that I took the offensive. I heard what he'd said. Write for fourteen year olds. I was never going to do that. And forget writing books for boys; I wasn't doing that either. No, I'd never write a series, which make more money. I'd love to live in NYC, but I had a job teaching at a university, a husband and four boys (for whom I would never write a book). And yet, I told *him*, I wanted him for my agent.

A couple of weeks later, Sheldon Fogelman called me, his voice animated and jovial. He loved my novel. He loved my letter. He loved me. We were best friends. We talked and laughed for an hour on the phone, (and I could actually speak). He told me I was the first client he had taken without meeting me in person. He told me I must come to New York, so we could meet.

In the spring, I went to Manhattan with friends, Francine and Helen Claire, who watched me press my red blazer in our hotel room the night before my appointment. The next day I walked down Fifth Avenue to mid-town on a sunny afternoon, took an elevator high in a tower to Sheldon Fogelman's front office, where I met the man himself. He was short, squarely built, and ebulliently good humored. Did he hug me? He did on later visits. He introduced me to Marcia Wernick, a slim, warm, petite woman, who would become my agent. They ushered me into Fogelman's office. From his window, I saw the Statue of Liberty in the distance. They talked to me for a couple of hours about *me* without taking a phone call, except one: it was Maurice Sendak.

I sat listening to this short conversation. I belonged to the same literary agency as Maurice Sendak. I was where the wild things were.

On the walk back to the hotel, I thought of all the years I had longed to be connected to NYC even if I couldn't live there. I had a NY publisher and now I had a NY agent. I had Maurice Sendak to brag about. I'm pretty sure I hummed, *New York, New York! If you can make it there, you'll make it anywhere.*

Best day of my life. Absolutely.

Note: If you have original sources such as letters, notes, journals or even emails, then by all means use them in your memoir, either as partial quotes or in full quotes when appropriate. The same goes for drawings and photos.

ANN'S TURN

So my best day ever happened when I went to New York and talked for hours with my new agent, who only interrupted our conversation when Maurice Sendak called.

Oh wait! I think that's Louise's best day ever. (Sorry, Louise. I didn't mean to appropriate your memory—it's just that I want your best day ever for myself. It's a really, really good one).

As you can probably tell I'm stalling a little. Best day ever? I'm having a hard time pinpointing one—was it the Christmas I received Chatty Cathy who said, "I love you," the first time I pulled her string? Or when my cat Sam had kittens behind the freezer in our garage? Or when Mark Bowen asked me to skate with him at the roller rink when we were in the sixth grade?

Was it that night in Paris when I thought that I was in love with a boy who I usually considered a friend? Or the moment I realized I was actually in love with the boy who became my husband? Or the minutes after giving birth when a new baby was pressed against my chest? Or the days when I met my babies' babies for the very first time?

This isn't to say my life is so awesome that all I have are Best Days Ever. No. No, no, and hell no.

But I've placed many small moments like the ones I've mentioned in a sort of mental memory box as though they were bits of sea glass. Moments that give me joy and occasionally peace when I examine them against the rough skin of my palm.

YOUR TURN

What shows up in your mental memory box? Write it down: Best. Day. Ever. And go for it. Or if you want to mix things up, write this down: Worst. Day. Ever. Then go for that one too. Speaking of worst days ever—sometimes people are reluctant to write about their hard stuff. They worry about sounding too negative or hurting loved ones. And sometimes they just don't want to revisit painful memories.

Bear in mind, however, that everyone has hard stuff and sometimes writing about your challenges is more inspiring to readers than celebrating your blessings. Just a thought.

CHAPTER 9

Surprised By Your Own History

ANN'S TURN

It happens. You think you know all you can possibly know about your immediate family, and, surprise, you find an untold story or a new version of an old story. Sometimes, it's funny and sometimes it makes your universe spin.

My grandmother's sisters, Bea and Blanche, were about as opposite as two great-aunts can be. Bea was all HEY, AIN'T LIFE GRAND? And Blanche was all WHERE'S THE NEAREST OVEN SO I CAN STICK MY HEAD IN IT?

Also, Blanche is the one who sat on Bea's Happy Halibut that time at the mall. I took them to buy some fish and chips and when we sat down we were missing an order. We discovered, finally, that Blanche was sitting on it. As you can see for yourself, that aunt was just no fun at all.

Anyway, my parents and I recently went to a family viewing where a very kind older woman asked who I was.

"I'm Patti Edwards' daughter," I told her.

"What's your name?" she asked.

"Ann Cannon."

"Oh," she said. "Were you adopted then?"

After we straightened that bit out, the woman's elderly husband told me he was Blanche's nephew and did I know that Blanche had been a good athlete. And then he said about the last thing I would have ever expected someone to say about my Aunt Blanche.

"She was a champion pole-vaulter."

I immediately texted this conversation to my brother Jimmy.

JIM: I didn't even know pole-vaulting was invented back then.

ME: The only thing that would have been more surprising to learn is that she'd been a champion pole-dancer.

JIM: This could create a whole new line of jokes. Why did Aunt Blanche choose the pole vault as an event?

ME: Why?

JIM: The 100-yard dash in a prairie skirt was too hard.

Bertie Wooster was right. Aunts are nothing if not surprising.

LOUISE'S TURN

Years ago, at a Copier (koh-PEER, not the Xerox machine) family reunion with all the Dutch aunts and uncles, I sat next to Tante Jans, my mother's oldest sister. She told me she had just translated Opoe's (my maternal grandmother) memoir. She patted a manuscript she had with her.

Opoe wrote a memoir? The only writing I had ever seen of hers was a one-page statement she wrote about her faith in the Mormon Church. As far as I knew, that was all she'd ever written about herself.

"Why haven't I ever seen this memoir?" I asked Tante Jans.

Her head drew close to mine as she whispered, "Well, there are things in there we didn't think the children should read."

I was pushing fifty, and was one of those "children."

"Like what?" I asked.

She leafed through the manuscript and handed it to me opened to a specific page. I strained to read an awkwardly translated Opoe. Like most people of her generation, Opoe had to have her teeth pulled in her early thirties and was fitted with false teeth. At home, she looked in the mirror and saw that the teeth made her beautiful. She felt vain, and vanity was a sin. The one thing my Bible-reading

Opoe never wanted to be was a sinner. The knowledge of her own vanity made her wretched.

So, she threw her teeth into the piet-burning stove and went toothless. *If thy right hand offend thee, cut it off.*

I would have stood in front of the mirror for a week, smiling at myself. Maybe a month. I would not have been able to pull myself away from that mirror. My teeth make me look beautiful. Saints be praised! I also felt like Nebuchadnezzar, King of Babylon: "weighed in the balance and found wanting," when compared to my "righteous" grandmother.

Later, at home, lying in bed, I got angry. What about chewing your food? What about the expense of those teeth? What is wrong with being beautiful? Beauty sluffs off all too quickly anyway. Turn around, and your head looks like a dried apple with a perfect set of ivories. Wasn't her action a wee bit neurotic? Dared I make this observation of a beloved and legendary grandmother?

Back at the picnic table with Tante Jans, I wanted to read Opoe's account of the death of the first twin girl, the six-year old Geertje. It proceeded pretty much the way I had heard it from my mother. Geertje died of tuberculosis. As soon as he heard, the minister of the Dutch Reformed Church in the village of Breukelen, whom Opoe had accused of misreading the Bible, walked to her house and told her the child was going to Hell, because Opoe hadn't had her baptized. Distraught with grief, and vulnerable, Opoe held onto her dead daughter for twenty-four hours, hoping to save her from burial and Hell.

I knew this story all too well. What was new was Opoe's opaque reference to the story of the daughter of Jairus in the *New Testament*. I pointed at it and asked Tante Jans what it meant. She shrugged her shoulders. No idea.

I remembered the daughter of Jairus only vaguely and looked it up in the Gospel of Mark. Jairus was one of the rulers of the synagogue, who "besot Jesus greatly." Telling him: "My little daughter lieth at the point of death; I pray thee, come and lay thy hands on her, that she may be healed; and she shall live." Jesus goes with him, but before he can reach Jairus's daughter, he is interrupted by the woman with the issue of blood, who touches the hem of his garment and is healed, because "thy faith hath made thee whole."

The story then returns to the daughter of Jairus where a messenger arrives to say, "Thy daughter is dead; why trouble the master any further?"

Jesus hears this and says, "Be not afraid, only believe."

When they approach the house, there is weeping and wailing. Jesus asks, "Why make ye this ado, and weep? The damsel is not dead, but sleepeth."

The crowd laughs at him, but he leads the mother and father into the house and takes the girl by the hand and says, "Damsel, I say unto thee, arise."

"And straightway the damsel arose and walked."

Opoe only wrote "the daughter of Jairus" into the memoir without further comment. What I see is one story, the daughter of Jairus, a faith healing, interrupted by a second story of a faith healing, the woman with the issue of blood. Two messages: "Thy faith hath made thee whole," and "Be not afraid, only believe."

What, I wondered, would Opoe be thinking while holding onto her dead daughter? What would a woman, who threw her teeth into the fire to save herself from sin, be thinking? How the daughter of Jairus had been healed? How the woman with the issue of blood had been healed? And possibly, she thought that she had not had enough faith to save her own daughter—a thought that would have made for a very dark night of the soul indeed.

Last year, I returned to the Netherlands and sat in Opoe's Dutch Reformed Church in Breukelen on a Sunday morning. I sang with the other worshippers accompanied by a stunning pipe organ. I listened to the slim and kind preacher talk to us of forgiveness and love. I thought then that Opoe was a part of her time and place, as was her unkind minister. They have been swept away with time's broom. The people in this new Breukelen know a truth that I have yet to learn completely: we are all equal in the sight of God, and what happened long ago no longer matters. I can forgive them both and hope that, sometime, I will be able to forgive even myself.

YOUR TURN

If you'd been a champion pole-vaulter in your youth, wouldn't you want people to know? Why not make a list of things people don't know about you? Did you sneak into movies? Have a crush on a boy with the cracking voice, who sat behind you in seventh-grade math? Win a ribbon at the state fair for your salsa? When you finish with your list, encourage the people in your life to make their own lists too.

CHAPTER 10

Places That Delighted or Repulsed You

LOUISE'S TURN

Writing about place is describing where the events of your life happened. It is writing about the house where you grew up, the ditch of running water in front of that house where you chased the odd ball that rolled into the fast current before it disappeared under the street at the intersection. It is Grandma's house with the chicken coop and the outhouse with the threatening hornets. It's the ramshackle trailer, where you spent summer vacation at Fish Lake. It's the elementary school lunch room that served up tuna on toast with canned peas.

The summer before second grade (1950), we moved into a brick house with a Victorian pattern, built in 1916. It had a large front facing window anchored with two slim windows, a modest wrap-around wooden porch with pink climbing roses blooming on a trellis. The house next door on the west side was identical. Houses on either side were no more than ten feet apart. Early mornings, Virginia Garrett practiced a limited version of *Grieg's Piano Concerto*, which wafted from her dining room into my bedroom window. Our house smelled a combination of nutmeg, Johnson's floor wax and electrical tape.

Another day, I might have chosen to write about the kitchen, but now it is the vestibule I want to write about. Did we—a Dutch immigrant family—actually call it the vestibule? Wouldn't we call it the front hall? I don't know anyone else who calls their front hall "the vestibule." I Googled "vestibule" in the middle of writing this paragraph and found that the word in Dutch is "de vestibule." Who knew? I stopped speaking Dutch at about eight or nine, so if I ever knew, I had long forgotten. "Vestibule" was a carry-over from Dutch.

Writing makes you smarter.

The vestibule was an eight-foot square front hall between the front door of the house, which had an oval glass in it, and the door leading into the house, in this case, the dining room, which was wide and also served as the hallway into the kitchen straight ahead. It had a soft wood floor covered with a utilitarian brown carpet for foot wiping. It was wallpapered. I mean that old wallpaper that really was paper, slightly textured, with small print almost indistinguishable from a beige color. A print that shy, modest people might pick. If it said anything, it was, "Welcome to my humble but clean house."

Every spring my mother took a fist of Play-Doh substance and rubbed off the coal dust from the wallpaper. I remember helping her until I lost interest, which surely would have been under five minutes. I may have tried sculpting a face from it. My point is, she kept the vestibule sparkling. There were no boots. No coats hanging from wall hooks. No table with keys and lost gloves. Occasionally, my sisters and I played jacks in there with the dining room door open. Family members always used the back door.

When I began dating Tom, Mother no longer had to clean the wallpaper, because by then we had a gas furnace. Tom and I "lingered" in the vestibule before saying good-bye. He would lean back, his head resting on the pristine wallpaper, and I would lean into him. Lots of leaning.

Over several months, a round, greasy spot appeared on the wallpaper where Tom's head rested. When I first saw it, I put my hand to my mouth to cover a gasp. Mother fought grease like a Viking pillaging a village, using her unusual upper body strength.

And now my boyfriend had violated her wallpaper. I was indirectly responsible. Did we confess to her? Surely she would have noticed. She noticed every fingerprint on a door frame.

She didn't care. "It's Tom's head, and I love Tom," she said. The stain stayed for years. Tom would say, "I see you still love Tom," and she would give him a playful slug to his arm, which meant, yes, she loved him to pieces.

Years later, when she developed Alzheimer's Disease and had forgotten most people's names, Tom went to make breakfast for my parents three mornings a week. He'd enter the back door and my father would say, "Do you know who that is?" She would smirk and said in a loud voice, "Tom Plummer!" Then as he fried eggs, careful to save the yokes, she would sneak behind him and break each one with a spatula and giggle like a girl.

ANN'S TURN

I recently asked my husband which places he'd like to haunt after he dies.

> HUSBAND: Wow. This conversation has suddenly taken a weird turn.

But I persisted because I think it's a good question. The answer says a lot about who you are (were) and what you value (valued.)

(Sorry about the past tense thing going on there. I don't mean to be morbid.)

Anyway, my husband finally said he'd haunt our house. Not in a bad Amityville Horror kind of way, but in a friendly hey-y'all-I'm-just-checking-in kind of way. His answer didn't surprise me, frankly, because my husband loves our house. And by house, I don't mean "home" with all that word's connotations. No. I mean he loves our actual brick and mortar house.

Why? Probably because he's done so much of the work on it himself—from painting walls to putting up sheet rock to crafting a fireplace mantel out of cherry wood to staining and varnishing floors to laying tile. You get the picture, right?

I think all that hard physical labor would put me off on a place—not unlike a stay at a prison farm or perhaps a Soviet gulag. But sweat has only served to seal the love deal with Ken—to make our house beyond dear to him. He owns it the way he owns his skin and bones, because that's what the house is to him. Skin and bones. An extension of his physical self.

So which places do I want to haunt?

I think I'd start with Hawaii.

Hawaii! Seriously, what a gig for ghost!

But my reasons are personal and not just because Hawaii is—you know—Hawaii. Hawaii was the first big-time-in-your-dreams-place I ever visited. I went with my parents, and while we were there, I turned sixteen. We went to a supper club in Honolulu—so glam! Also fancy—where someone told the performer-in-residence, Don Ho, that a certain Haole girl wearing a neon orange muumuu in the audience was having a birthday. So Don Ho made me get up on the stage with him. And he serenaded me while my parents looked on, wondering (no doubt) why they'd ever let me buy that neon orange muumuu.

So that's where I want to go. Back to Hawaii . And while I'm there, I want to see myself and my parents feeling the kiss of tropical air on our skins for the very first time—with so, so much life ahead of us still.

YOUR TURN

What places would you haunt? And why? What are the places that haunted you, nurtured you, and made you feel safe? What are the places that made you feel heroic, adventuresome, or scared and even crazy? Try to describe "your place" using all five senses: sight, sound, touch, smell and taste; and then, having done that, don't forget to include yourself in that place. Remember you're not just describing a place, you're describing *you* in that place. It's a story of you in a specific landscape.

CHAPTER 11

List-o-mania

ANN'S TURN

Are you the kind of person who loves to make lists?

If so, consider writing about your life by generating lists that tell your reader something about you. In other words, list yourself! For example, you could make a list of the books that have meant the most to you and then annotate it. My list of books would look something like this:

The Little Black Puppy by Charlotte Zolotow—This is the first book I read cover-to-cover by myself. The sense of achievement I felt when I reached the final page stays with me still.

Little Women by Louisa May Alcott—I read this the summer between my fifth- and sixth-grade years, stretched out on a grassy slope beside our house in Edgemont. I completely identified with tomboy Jo March. Because of Jo I wanted to be a writer and have a bunch of boys. Which I did! (Louise did the full Jo March, however. She had boys, became a writer, AND married herself a German professor. Oh, Louise. You're such an over-achiever).

A Wrinkle in Time by Madeleine L'Engle—I read this book in the sixth grade. I was intrigued by the idea that Meg's supposed weakness—her temper—also became her greatest strength. Books for children can be full of adult truths.

Exodus by Leon Uris—I read this book in the seventh grade, and as a result I decided to join the Israeli army and devote my life to protecting the modern state of Israel. Also, there was kissing in the book. Bonus!

The Fellowship of the Ring by J.R.R. Tolkien—I bought this book on a hot afternoon in Pomona, California while I was waiting for my football coach father, who was recruiting a player at the time. I started reading it on a bench outside the dreary little drugstore where I'd bought it and was oddly smitten by the epic tale of little men with hairy feet. Who knew?

Kristin Lavransdatter by Sigrid Undset—I read this stunning trilogy when I was supposed to be reading something else in graduate school. At the time I especially related to the daughter/father relationship in the first book, because I loved my dad as much as Kristin loved hers.

The Madonnas of Leningrad by Debra Dean—What stirred me most about this book was its theme, the idea that love and art can transcend something as brutal as the historic siege of Leningrad.

All the Light We Cannot See by Anthony Doerr—I must love books about the second world war, because I have more than a few of them on my all time favorites lists—*The Forgotten Garden* by Helen Humphreys and *Prince of the Clouds* by Gianni Riotta, for example—but reading *All the Light* transported me to a field covered with snow in Germany and a beach pounded by waves in France as the world went up in flames. I read this book at a time when a tiny part of my world felt like it was going up in flames, too, and for that reason alone my heart will always own this book.

See how it works? A list like this says something about who you are and what you value. Here are some other possible topics for list-making. Be sure to write a sentence or two about each thing you list.

Jobs I've held
Past addresses
Places I've visited
Places I'd like to visit
Compliments I receive on a regular basis

Things I can't live without
Experiences I wish I'd had when I was young
Experiences I wish I hadn't had
People who've influenced me
Best advice I've ever received (and from whom)
Things that Energize Me
Worries I no longer worry about
Houses I've lived in
Pet Peeves
My Happy Places and (of course)
Books I've Read

LOUISE'S TURN

Ann suggests you write a couple of sentences next to each item on the list, but I think some lists can stand alone. Here's a couple of them

Things I have done but will never do again:

- eat at Chuck E. Cheese
- visit Disneyland
- ride a Ferris wheel
- play chess
- take a bus cross-country
- dye my hair
- buy a dog
- have a baby
- have a period
- eat a Twinkie
- go on a blind date or any date, for that matter
- buy an American car
- read Proust
- read Nicholas Sparks or Danielle Steele
- wear shorts
- hitchhike or pick up hitchhikers
- pee in my car (how can I actually guarantee this?)

- get up at 5 a.m. to do anything
- smoke a cigarette/cigar
- watch *Somewhere in Time*

Things I shouldn't do but probably will anyway:

- cut my own hair
- sew something
- let the grandchildren guzzle Dr. Peppers
- skip church
- tell a Polish joke
- complain/whine/sulk
- scratch until it bleeds
- wear Tom's underwear when I run out of my own
- look at myself in a magnified mirror
- stay up past midnight
- skip the sunscreen
- leave my clothes on the floor
- mix whites and colors
- curse
- dance in my undies on the back porch
- take sleeping pills
- ask Tom who he'll marry when I die

Dark Fortune Cookies—(my son, Edmund, my husband, Tom, and I made up this list one punch-drunk night, because we thought regular fortune cookies were too boring; our cookies would be the highest quality chocolate):

- You will lose a nipple in a freak accident in a shoe store.
- You will write a bestselling book about the 20 years you spent in prison in Yemen.
- Toe fungus is in your future.
- Watch out for your toaster.
- Your doctor is lying. There is no cure.
- Don't worry. You won't need your thumbs anyway.
- You have no lucky numbers.

- You're going to need braces again.
- Make sure you're buried with a flashlight in your casket.
- Blood in your stools on Friday.
- Better take baby steps this week.
- Your father isn't your father.
- Don't open your door to anyone the last week of the month.
- All your children will look like Yogi Berra
- Dead man walking.
- You ARE the tooth fairy.
- Walk with a limp on Monday.
- Kiss all the princes you want, you'll still be a frog.
- Go ahead: step on that crack!

YOUR TURN

Once you have the idea of lists, you won't be able to stop listing. They're addictive, and they say a lot about you in short order. In fact, you *could* write a whole memoir using only lists.

CHAPTER 12

What You Ate

ANN'S TURN

I hate to admit this, but okay fine. I was a Princess Diana groupie. I bought every magazine known to man if her picture was on the cover. I lined my shelf with books about her, including *The Royal Family Pop-Up Book*, which features Corgis that jump when you pull the tabs. Of course I had her haircut, and I even wore collars with bow ties, just like she did.

My mother didn't get it. If I was going to have a crush on a modern-day princess, why not choose Princess Grace of Monaco. Now there was a real princess, according to my mother. But that's the point. Diana was a woman of my generation. I could identify with her and her taste, just as my mother identified with Princess Grace and today's young mothers see themselves in Kate Middleton.

I'm over my thing for Diana and the Royal Family now. Mostly. But I have to confess that when the cookbook *Eating Royally: Recipes and Remembrances From a Palace Kitchen* was published a few years ago, I bought it. Why? Because it was written by Darren McGrady, private chef to Princess Diana.

I haven't cooked much from it, but I do like to read the little annotations: "Eggs drumkilbo was the Queen Mother's favorite and one we always put on the menu when she came to stay. It was also served at the wedding breakfast of Princess Anne and Captain Mark Phillips in 1973."

Seriously, I can die happy now that I know what Princess Anne ate on her wedding day.

My own Queen Mother also annotates her recipes. My favorite appears on a recipe for her killer chocolate chip chocolate cake. Here's what she wrote: "BYU played SMU in the 1980 Holiday Bowl. SMU led the whole game. With three minutes and 56 seconds left, BYU scored 21 points and won the game. YIPPEE! I wrote a note (after the game) to my friend, Cindy Meyer. Her husband, Ron, was the coach of SMU. I told her I was glad BYU won, but that I felt deeply for her.

"Cindy wrote back and said that friendship was more important than football. To prove her point she sent me her favorite recipe."

Do you see where I'm going with this? One way to write memoir is by compiling your favorite recipes and telling the story behind them—who liked this dish and why, when you served it, where you got it. Laurie Colwin, the short story writer, did this to great effect in her charming book *Home Cooking*.

Food for thought, right? (See what I just did there?!)

And speaking of recipes, here's my mother's chocolate chocolate chip cake recipe. Don't tell her I've shared it. She and Cindy Meyer will kill me.

Patti's Famous Chocolate Chip Cake

1 box yellow cake mix

1 small box of instant chocolate pudding

½ cup sugar

¾ cup oil

¾ cup water

4 eggs

8 oz. sour cream

1 small package chocolate chips

MIX: cake mix, pudding mix, and sugar

ADD: oil and water

BEAT: w/ wooden spoon 1 egg at a time

FOLD IN: sour cream and chocolate chips.

BAKE: in a greased and floured tube pan at 350 for 50-60 minutes

COOL: one hour before removing from pan

LOUISE'S TURN

Foods my Mother Fed Me—a List

- Vienna sausages
- Spam
- Deviled ham
- hot dogs split in half and fried
- chocolate sprinkles on toast (very Dutch)
- Cream of Wheat made with whole milk—sugar on top (We called it "pap" which is porridge in Dutch).
- Dunford doughnuts
- canned green beans
- brown bread (homemade)
- butter for Mother; margarine for everyone else
- oleybollen and appelflappen (on New Year's Eve)
- raisin cake at Christmas
- vegetable soup with meatballs floated on top (must haves: cauliflower and celery tops)
- pea soup with leeks (begin with a ham bone)
- meatballs made with Holland Rusk and one teaspoon nutmeg added
- Saturday night pancakes. Each one filled the whole frying pan. How did she flip them?
- Sunday pot roasts with gravy, slowly simmered in a black Dutch pot with a blue interior, brought from the Netherlands.
- cauliflower in a white sauce I've never been able to replicate
- rice cooked in a pressure cooker served for dessert with sugar on top
- potatoes, potatoes, potatoes! Boiled.

- the best hot chocolate on the planet. Here's the recipe:

For one cup hot chocolate, create a heavy syrup by mixing 1 teaspoon cocoa, 4 teaspoons sugar and mix with a tiny bit of water to make a syrup (too much water will spoil it). Add this syrup to ¾ cup of heated whole milk (it won't be as good with less than whole milk—this is no time to diet). Stir. Top with whipped cream. I want to die while drinking this hot chocolate. Everyone in my family knows how to make it. If you want to make it for a crowd, the recipe is the same: one part cocoa to four parts sugar, add water, and ¾ cup milk for each person. Thank you, Mother.

YOUR TURN

No doubt you could structure an entire book-length memoir around recipes and memories of food. Start with a single recipe and move on from there. You can organize it later. Remember to schedule breaks for yourself, because writing about food will make you hungry.

CHAPTER 13

Life is But a Dream

ANN'S TURN

The last time I ever saw my grandmother in this life, I was angry with her. I'd just had a baby so the hormones surging through my sleep-deprived body were all big and blowzy. My husband and I were also loading up a van to move us, our five children, three dogs, one cat, and a cockatiel to upstate New York.

As always my grandmother was there, helping me. And as always my grandmother was driving me crazy. I loved my grandmother, but there were times when her desire to help and her insistence that she was right about everything made me nuts—especially when I was already feeling stressed.

So, I snapped at her. Then I took off in that U-Haul in a huff.

Six weeks later she was dead.

It's hard to describe the grief and guilt I felt when I received the news. More than anything, I wanted to have a re-do of our last moments together.

A few weeks later, I had a dream. I dreamed I walked into an empty room in the church and found her sitting on a chair, waiting for me.

"I was wondering when you would show up," I said to her.

She shrugged. "Well, you know me."

After that exchange, the two of us walked outside onto the church grounds. The grass was long and sweet and moist with dew. The sun was butter. Overhead, a flotilla of black angels filled the sky, chanting their joy.

My grandmother linked her arm through mine then, and the two of us walked in companionable silence through the grass that kissed our ankles while listening to the rolling music.

Most of my dreams are of the grubby, petty variety. I can't find my class. Store clerks laugh at me when I try on a swimsuit. I trip on a sprinkler head and twist my ankle. But when I awoke from this dream, my heart was filled with peace.

And over the years, *that* has become the last memory I have of my grandmother here on earth.

LOUISE'S TURN

You'll have to decide for yourself whether you or members of your family have had a dream or a series of dreams that you want to include in a memoir. Ann's dream of her grandmother transcends the physical world and offers a more benevolent closure to their relationship.

Years ago, my friend, Sandy, had a similar dream. Her mother had died and Sandy was not only bereft but confounded. She had always believed in a Christian afterlife, but now confronted with her mother's absence, she questioned her previous assumptions. Did her mother still exist in some form and where was she? What was she doing?

Months passed, and then Sandy had this dream: her mother, looking young and healthy and content, sat at a desk writing in a notebook. When she sensed Sandy's presence, she looked up and said, "You can't believe how different it is here. It is so *different!*"

That was it. No delicious details comparing earthly life and afterlife. The important thing for Sandy was that her mother existed somewhere. She didn't care about details. In the morning, she called her brother, who lived in another state, to tell him about her dream of their mother, only to find that he had had the exact same dream the night before.

Once I was telling these kinds of anecdotes to my father, who said, "We don't have those dreams in our family." As if to say, *we're Dutch, we don't need Novocain. We don't need an afterlife*, although he believed in one.

Did *he* come to me in a dream? Yes, and I was not expecting him. My brother and sisters as adults were gathered in the family home playing games in the dining room, when the door from the vestibule opened, and my father appeared looking mid-fortyish, wearing his suit and raincoat and a hat as if he were returning from a church meeting. His face was cheerful, his eyes mischievous and shining. "Hi," he said, and laughed that little heh heh heh.

I cried out, "You're dead!" and woke myself up. You're dead, as in how can you be here in my dream all realistic-like? How can you be here like your old self? Yes, my father came to me in a dream and scared the liver out of me, because that's pretty much the way we Dutch people relate to each other. I can hear him say to my mother, "Got her that time!"

My dream of Mother was more bizarre: she came, wearing roller-skates and looking determined. She, too, was a younger version of herself. She wore a summer dress and stood at the top of State Street in Salt Lake City and pushed off down what is a very steep hill like a Dutch speed skater. I stayed at the top of the hill, anxious and useless, yelling, "Mother stop! Mother, you're going too fast! Mother!"

She yelled, "Wheee!" all the way down.

Important? Compelling? Just a dream? My parents live in my bones, in my blood, in every breath I take. They haunt me to my marrow.

YOUR TURN

What dreams have made a difference to you? Write about the important ones. Give them a shape before they slip away.

CHAPTER 14

Hypochondria, Sickness, Insanity, and Death

LOUISE'S TURN

I had the following childhood illnesses: diphtheria, whooping cough, measles, chicken pox and mumps. I didn't break any bones, but I wanted a broken bone in elementary school, because it was so cool to have a plaster cast on your arm for all your friends to sign. I definitely didn't want polio, except for a brief hour when I visited the brand new Primary Children's Hospital in Salt Lake City in the early fifties with its giant cartoon figures painted on the walls, and a pool for paralyzed children to float in. I liked cartoons and swimming pools.

On the mental health side, I had major anxiety, something I wasn't able to diagnose or articulate until well into adulthood, when I went into therapy. From ages seven to nine, I was phobic about wind. I was terrified of being blown away. I checked the trees on my block to see if the leaves trembled; if they did, I'd go inside and lie down on my bed.

Once when there was a violent windstorm in the afternoon, my mother and sister Janie, walked toward my school to meet me and found me hugging a light pole, fearful of proceeding any further. The wind absorbed my every waking moment for two years. Even as

I write, I have a growing knot in my stomach. I was shamed out of this fear when I was nine years old, came out of church on a windy day and sprinted home in terror. Behind me, Karen Forbush broke into hee-hawing and shouted, "Look, Louise is afraid of the wind!"

Humiliation is more frightening than any phobia. I stopped fearing wind. Karen needs to come back into my life to laugh at the new fears I manage to conjure up for myself. Imagination isn't always better than knowledge.

Then there was the odd rash on either side of my lips when I was seven. That year, Sears, Roebuck and Company was the playground for my brother, Gerard, and me. One day they were giving away free popsicles at the bottom of the escalator in the basement, and we got in line for ours. A woman in an apron stood behind a table, picking the popsicles out of an ice chest and handing them to customers. She handed one to Gerard, but held back when she saw me. "You've already had one," she said. "I can see the grape stains at the side of your mouth." She gestured me off with the popsicle in her hand and gave it to the next person in line.

Second grade was the year of the sty. I had one every other week and would be sent home, because stys were highly contagious. This irritated my mother, because I wasn't sick enough to warrant being underfoot at home. I don't ever remember seeing another child with a sty, so sending me home must have been highly effective.

I had chronic nosebleeds as a child. One night, I filled a diaper (held to my nose) with blood. That's when my mother hauled me off to the doctor. He checked me out and said to my mother, "If this continues, she'll have to have her nose cauterized." He explained that this was a procedure that burned off the weak blood vessels with a hot needle. "It hurts," he said.

Sitting there on the examining table, with two adults hovering over me, I knew I never ever wanted to have my nose cauterized. The nosebleeds had to stop. And they did. They stopped cold.

Two childhood scars: one between my thumb and index finger of my right hand, where Gerard slashed me with a knife in Opa's apple orchard. Adults wrapped my hand and I rode on the back of someone's bike to the doctor in Breukelen, who gave me a lecture about not playing with knives while he stitched up my hand. Even at age five, I bristled at the lecture. I already knew not to play with knives. Talk to Gerard, why don't you.

The second scar above the left elbow happened on the day I got the mumps, when I fell against an old stove that heated my porch bedroom. That second-degree burn was more traumatic than having mumps. It blistered and leaked and throbbed until it grew a thick crust of scab and left me with a wide, tight scar as a reminder that I shouldn't fall against hot stoves.

The word "allergy" was unknown in our house. Every spring, I developed a dry, choking cough that I later realized must have been a yearly allergy. I don't remember knowing the word "allergy" until I married Tom, whose entire childhood was about allergies and quack cures.

Even death was not addressed in our family. The summer before I turned ten, my sister, Joyce, who had been a healthy, pink, laughing baby, died at age four months of some vague respiratory illness. She had been sick for a few weeks, and the doctor visited our house regularly to monitor her illness. She must have had penicillin—this was 1952. I do remember my parents' concern, and all seven of us suspended over her bassinet, which Mother had decorated in lace in the European fashion.

The doctor may have suggested using a humidifier to ease Joyce's breathing, and my father, with doting enthusiasm, placed a plank across the bassinet and set the humidifier on it, so the steam floated above her head. The humidifier turned out to be defective and later that night, spat burning drops of scalding water on the baby's face.

Joyce cried, inconsolable.

But she did recover, and her breathing grew more normal. One Saturday night, all seven of us stood around her crib, relieved, as she smiled and giggled at us. "She's getting better," someone said aloud. We repeated it. "She's getting better.

The next morning, Gerard came to my sleeping porch. "Joyce died," he said.

I didn't believe him. "That's not funny," I said.

"No, she did," he said and disappeared.

Then my father appeared with red swollen eyes and repeated the news. I believed.

I got out of bed. Mother was not up. Daddy must have been with her in their bedroom. Where was Joyce? I wandered through the house. A folded blanket lay on the couch, and I looked underneath it to see if she might be there. Where was she? What had they done with her?

We six children were packed off next door to the Garretts' house for the day. Mrs. Garrett made up a platter of tuna fish sandwiches on white bread, which tasted like cake to me. We sat around a table in the back yard. I ate one sandwich after another trying to fill a hole that had developed inside of me. I must have eaten a half-dozen sandwiches. That night, I threw up. I threw up the next day. I was too sick to attend the funeral. Mourners came to the house for refreshments, and I sat in the living room listening to adults chattering and murmuring with my aunts.

That evening, we went to the cemetery where Joyce's grave was covered with large bouquets of roses and gladiolas. Someone snapped a photo. That was it: the death of my sister.

That school year, I was not the teacher's pet. I was just one of the average kids, sitting blankly at my desk, third row from the window.

ANN'S TURN

For a long time when I remembered that year I spent in bed, I thought of how I felt—afraid, isolated, bored, curious about death, delighted by small gifts and brief visits. But lately I've been thinking about my parents and how they felt about that year, and so I've asked them to jot down some memories of that experience from their point of view. Here they are, LaVell and Pat Edwards in their own words.

My Father

I was an assistant football coach for BYU and a bishop on campus at the time of my daughter's illness. At that time one of the things I looked forward to at the end of the day or any time I had a spare moment was sitting by my daughter's bed and listening to the musical score from *West Side Story*. My daughter had a phonograph by her bed and the two of us would play the record over and over.

It was a glorious day when she was well and was able to get out of bed for two reasons. The main reason was that she was well. The other reason was I didn't have to listen to *West Side Story* anymore. By the time she was well, I wanted to take the record and the machine and toss them out of the window.

Today when I hear the musical score it brings back memories of being with my daughter. Just the two of us loving the music and each other.

My Mother

Nephritis wasn't a new word to me. I was well acquainted with it and its viciousness. My Aunt Winnie and my dear friend Joanne Marancic both died from nephritis. I knew about nephritis, and when Ann was diagnosed I was frightened and frantic. In fact I lived with fear for the whole year of her illness.

"Mama, how does it feel to die?" "Mama, can I take my toys to heaven?" Those two questions were asked a lot at the beginning of Ann's illness. Fortunately, those questions weren't answered. I know it was because many times a day my knees were bent and a quick prayer was said on her behalf.

Think how empty the world would have been without her! She has truly made it a better world because she has walked this earth. Maybe her illness has helped her to do this.

Ann

I asked my parents to write these paragraphs for me over lunch at David's Kitchen, a fine little Chinese restaurant in Salt Lake City. They went right home and wrote these for me. I cried a little when I read them. Because they have always been my parents—forever older and wiser than I am—I've sometimes forgotten how very young they were when illness struck our family.

But I have never forgotten their kindness.

YOUR TURN

Consider writing about how your family dealt with illness and death. Were you coddled when you were sick? Did your mother allow you to lie on the sofa and watch daytime television? Did she buy your treats? Bring you lunch? Or did she send you to school to tough it out?

If you had chronic illness in your family—if, for example, one parent was schizophrenic, or a sibling was autistic, or someone lingered with cancer—then an entire memoir might be focused on how you and individual members of your family handled it.

CHAPTER 15

Pick a Word, Any Word

ANN'S TURN

Here's a type of rush-writing that helps me get my writerly juices (sounds messy!) flowing when I feel inspired. I solicit nouns from my blog readers, and then for the next few days I do riffs on the nouns they send me. I follow the rules we've already laid out here—I write fast for a short period of time, and I don't look in the rear view mirror to see if what I've written is working. It's a fun, freeing experience—a little like shouting "Look Ma! No hands!" when you whiz past her on your bicycle (before you crash into the neighbor's mailbox). And the good news is that sometimes I've generated material I've later used in other contexts.

Let me give you an example.

One friend sent me the word "vampire" and this is what I wrote:

When I was growing up, one of the local TV stations—I think it may have been Channel 5—had a program on Friday nights called *Nightmare Theater,* which showed many B-horror movies featuring large lizards terrorizing Japanese people. It was an elementary school rite of passage to watch *Nightmare Theater.* It meant you were a) old enough to stay up past the ten o'clock news and b) brave enough to watch large lizards terrorizing Japanese people. In other words, you weren't a baby anymore.

I think I may have been eight or nine when I decided to stop being a baby. So I stayed up late one Friday night and watch my first *Nightmare Theater* with my dad who apparently decided to stop being a baby, too. The film was called *House of Dracula*, which not only involved vampires but also Wolfman, and a hunchback too. Good times!

It scared me. TO DEATH. It scared me right back to being a baby. At least where vampires are concerned. So it has been with a great deal of bewilderment that I have watched vampires turn into this century's Romantic Icons, causing ladies to get all swooney. I don't get it.

I think vampires (badda badda boom) suck.

Later, when I was looking for an idea I could turn into a column, I remembered this post. And, lo, it did become a column. And, also, lo, I did use some of the very same phrases I'd already turned, such as that one about *House of Dracula* featuring Wolfman and a hunchback, as well as vampires.

It must be said, however, that my mother was unhappy with that particular line. When I asked her why, she said I might make actual hunchbacks who read my column feel bad about themselves.

LOUISE'S TURN

Ann introduced me to this exercise, and the noun she used was "butter." It brought this memory of my mother to the forefront:

My mother was the only one in our large family who was allowed to eat butter. She had her own little plate of it, which we were not to touch. The rest of us had to eat margarine. I tasted her butter, and I wanted to it eat on my toast instead of margarine.

"No," Mother said.

"Why do you get to eat butter and we have to eat margarine?" I asked. (My life has been a long series of "why" questions).

Her answer: "Because I have a rheumatic heart."

I believed her for years, until I was in my twenties and lived in Cambridge, Mass. 02138 and realized one Sunday afternoon that her answer made no sense at all. I called her long-distance and said, "You lied to me about why you got to eat butter!"

She laughed hard, unrepentant. When she caught her breath, she said, "Butter was too expensive for a big family, but I can't stand margarine." Laugh, laugh, hoo-haw, laugh.

Never trust your mother.

YOUR TURN

Time for you to make a list of nouns. And to make things even more fun and spontaneous, take that list and cut it into word strips— one noun per paper. Then put all those lovely words in a basket or a fish bowl (preferably without a fish in it) so you can randomly draw a word on which to riff.

Here are some good nouns I've collected from friends over the years, if you need some help:

Apple	Umbrella	Queen	Aardvark
Quilt	Bicycle	Button	Castle
Riot	Cocoa	Dog	Delicacy
Restaurant	Snow	Education	Edamame
Shoes	Face	Fact	Gift
Tomato	Gargoyle	House	Heaven
Tornado	Intuition	Igloo	Jacks
Education	Jelly	Kite	Kitchen
Laundry	Lilacs	Mountain	Mess
Neck	Neaderthal	Opera	Outfield
Poodle	Pie		

CHAPTER 16

The Influential and the Nemeses

ANN'S TURN

In her book, *Making a Literary Life*, Carolyn See advises writers to make up a list of influential people in their life, along with a nemesis or two. The idea is that these individuals can inspire the creation of your memoir characters.

My Influential People:

- My dad: When I was three I told him I was going to marry him some day. He was my first serious crush. When I was little he taught me how to swim and wrestle and do cartwheels on the front lawn. Also, he laughed at my jokes. Who could resist?
- My mom: She was easily the best-looking woman on our street. I never ever doubted her love for us, but she could be moody sometimes, which baffled me as a kid and angered me as a teenager. And then one day I turned into the moody one with kids. Meanwhile, she turned into my best friend.
- My younger brother: Dude is the funniest guy ever. I love it when he pulls out the piano bench, lies on it stomach down, and does his imitation of a Macy's Thanksgiving Day balloon.

- The boy who shall remain nameless: I was madly in love with him from the sixth grade until the twelfth grade— AND HE NEVER NOTICED. What was so wrong with me that I could never get him to take a second look?
- Miss Nelson: My high school AP English teacher. A flamboyant dresser and an entertaining one-woman show. When we were reading *The Great Gatsby* she made the surprising announcement in class that "men like women who smolder." I've never forgotten that. I've also wondered if I smolder, and if there's an app on a smartphone that would let me know.
- Sally, Kathy and Nancy: If that book the *Ya-Ya Sisterhood* didn't annoy me so much, I would say these women are my Ya-Yas. Except without the growing-up-Catholic-in -Louisiana-and-drinking-too-much part. We have walked together rain or shine in the dark hours of the morning for thirty years.
- Louise Plummer: Do I need to explain?
- Ken Cannon: My Numero Uno Important Person. He looked like a hood with his thick black beard and greasy sweatshirt the summer we first met. I wasn't exactly smitten then—but I was interested. Later, we discovered each other when we had gone to the same elementary school, but apparently he had to grow some facial hair, and I had to get some hormones before I noticed. He sent off my first manuscript to Delacorte. He turned me into a novelist.

A Nemesis or Two:

This list changes. For awhile there I didn't like this mom whose son played basketball against my son. I wanted to challenge her to a hair-pulling fight at halftime and my money was on *me*. I used to have hair-pulling fights in my mind with Sarah Palin for awhile, too, so I guess in a way she was another nemesis. An imaginary nemesis, not unlike the Kardashians, who appear to be so busy taking selfies that they don't have time for real lives. But that's not my problem, is it?

No. My real nemesis is myself these days—primarily because I just won't get out of my own damn way.

LOUISE'S TURN

When you capitalize nemesis into Nemesis, you get the Greek goddess of retributive justice. What a colossal irony, because our family's only historical nemesis was Sam the Greek. My father never called him just old Sam, Sam the Landlord, or that damn Sam. No, it was always Sam the Greek.

As you can guess, "Greek" was not meant to be complimentary. It did not speak to those ancients, who created all that was good about western civilization. I doubt that my father was acquainted with any Greeks at all, ancient or modern, so Sam set the standard. My apologies to his progeny. If you recognize yourself, call me, and I'll take you to lunch.

The first house my parents rented after coming to America in 1948 was at 480 Wentworth Avenue in Salt Lake City, directly behind what was then known as St. Anne's orphanage, and I fretted that I never saw any children outdoors. I must have been raised with superstitions about Catholics, because I remember clearly thinking that the nuns kept the orphans locked up in the basement. (Mother once told me that they had considered putting me in Catholic preschool, but decided against it. I'd bet an old Dutch guilder that they were afraid I'd come home hailing Mary).

The house on Wentworth was a one-bedroom house with an outhouse in the back. It did have a large bathtub and a kitchen sink, but the water poured under the house. If we had to pee late at night, Mother let us do it in the tub. She rinsed it out with a red hose. If you had to go number two, it was out to the cranny, where the bees awaited you.

The rent was $15.00 a month.

My parents came into this forlorn little house with four and a half children. They painted it inside and out. My father replaced all the electrical fixtures, and because it had no heat, he put in a coal stove. They put up curtains. They tidied the yard. The one bedroom was furnished with two new bunk beds. A fold-up couch was placed in the living room along with a bassinet for the first American-born child, Teddy.

Sam the Greek lived on 5th East, and our back yards connected, separated by a chain link fence with trees of heaven jutting from its edges. He kept goats, which created a stench, but this did not stop my fascination with them. I leaned into the fence until I had diamond shapes welded into my forehead. Mother hated the goats, and the overwhelming odor that wafted across the yard suffusing her freshly hung laundry on the clothesline.

One summer afternoon a small group of children gathered out in front of Sam the Greek's house, where he tied empty tin cans to a stray dog's back legs. The dog was a large, emaciated, short-haired animal with sad brown eyes and a docile manner. It may have had a Weimaraner ancestor back in the 15th century. I was six and had no idea why an adult was tying cans to a dog's legs. Was this a party?

When the burly Sam finished tying more than a half-dozen cans, he took a switch from a tree and beat the dog's rump with all his strength. The dog howled and took off running, the cans clattering behind, the howling increasing with the dog's terror.

Sam growled a smutty laugh. We children wandered, helpless, toward home.

Gerard and I went to Forest Elementary School. We learned to ride bicycles and play "Fish." We walked along the train tracks and looked for frogs in the ditch. I stole three candy bars from a neighborhood grocer and found that my nervous system was not up to a life of crime. Daddy listened to the Salt Lake Bees games on the radio after work. Mother hid behind a chair when a stranger came to the front door and I was sent to say she wasn't home. We bought a '38 Chevy, the first part of my father's American dream.

That first year sped by, and it was time to renew the lease on the house. With all the improvements my parents had made, Sam the Greek, recognizing a more valuable property, raised the rent from $15.00 to $50.00 a month, a price my parents couldn't afford. I remember my friend, Julie, from next door, finding me at the edge of the neighborhood and breathlessly telling me that my father and Sam the Greek were yelling at each other across the back fence. By the time I got there, it was all over.

We had to move and move quickly. My parents found a temporary one-bedroom apartment a half block from Sears on Main Street in a building that was due for demolition. My father removed all the new fixtures he had put into the little house and brought them along to the apartment.

Sam the Greek sued him. My father's boss at the electrical company where he worked, offered to escort him to court and help him explain his position, which was: in Europe, people do take electrical fixtures with them from house to house. In America, you leave fixtures behind or replace them. The judge asked my father to replace the fixtures. No extra money was involved.

What my father said: "I should have painted the bugger's house black."

YOUR TURN

Remember Obi-wan Kenobi from *Star Wars*? In real life his name was Alec Guiness, and in addition to being a fine actor, Sir Alec was also an accomplished memoirist. His verbal portraits of the people he knew are small gems. Check out his book, *Blessings in Disguise,* and see for yourself. Write about someone who has been a nemesis or a plague in your life, or about someone who has had a positive influence.

CHAPTER 17

The Unsent Letter

LOUISE'S TURN

Dear Mother and Daddy,

The sisters and I play cards the first Monday of every month and we talk about you. Are your celestial ears ringing? Why don't the two of you join us one night, because we have questions.

I said, one night, that I had never heard the two of you argue more than once or twice, and it was always about Daddy being away too much. These fights were played off stage and weren't loud and ended with Mother red-eyed and sniffling.

"Whaaaat?" the sisters asked in unison, gawping. "They used to yell at each other all the time!" Toni said. Marilyn said she was afraid they would get divorced. Judy said, "I told them to stop once."

Parents of mine, I have no memory of you yelling at each other. Was I gone? Was this your middle-aged marriage playing itself out? What were you yelling about?

Tom and I had a big yelling fight once in our middle-aged marriage. It was a Sunday afternoon before dinner, and Tom had made a huge green salad for about fifty people (even though there were only six of us at the most). I attacked from behind and doused the salad with dressing. Glug. Glug. Glug.

He was livid. "It's takes two hours to make this salad, and you've ruined the whole thing for leftovers!"

"I don't like to mix a salad and its dressing on my plate," I said. Two hours, really?

"I made the salad, and I don't like wasting half of it." He seethed.

"I hate mixing on a plate!"

That was the subject of the argument and it got heated. I wanted to tear his skin off.

The boys sat in the dining room amazed at the savage quarrel about salad. Charles had just returned from a trip to California and thought he had come home to divorcing parents.

Another time, Tom and I hissed at each other across a booth at the Brick Oven in Provo when our youngest son, Sam, was with us. He must have been a Freshman at BYU. "Will you two just stop it! We're in a restaurant! Stop it!" Sam scolded. We were cowed into a sulking silence.

Hey, parents of mine, did your parents argue too? About salad?

There was never any doubt in my mind that the two of you loved each other. Never.

It won't surprise you to hear that Tom and I are still married. We learned to take part of the large salad and mix it in a smaller bowl for six people. The rest was saved for another day.

What's it like where you are? Tell me it's not a long dreary church meeting. I'd rather molder in the grave.

What's it like? Come back and tell us. Don't be so Dutch. Drop a clue.

ANN'S TURN

Wow. Talk about a great idea. Some of my favorite novels are written in the epistolary form. (If you haven't read *Dear Committee Members* by Julie Schumacher—a story told entirely in a series of cranky letters of recommendation—you should. Immediately! And you're welcome.) So why not take this venerated fictional format and use if for memoir.

My letter—one I truly wish I could send—goes something like this.

Dear Kevin,

I hope you don't remember me from our high school days. But I'm guessing, sadly, that you probably do.

So I ended up having five sons and the oldest had an experience when he was sixteen that made me so crazy mad I could almost feel my hair catch on fire. I wasn't mad at him, btw. I was angry with the sixteen year old girl he'd asked out on a date but who stood him up and thereby humiliated him to the core. I'm not sure he really ever got over that experience—at least not until high school and maybe even the first few years of college were in his rear view mirror. I used to fantasize about telling that girl off and telling her that while everybody else thought she was fabulous—A straight-A student! A star soccer player! A class officer! An active member of the church!—I thought she was a cold-hearted little brat.

Even after my son got over it, I hung onto my anger at this sixteen year-old girl.

When it comes to holding a grudge, I have few peers as it turns out.

Anyway. That's not the point. The point is that for some reason I thought of you one day. How you had a crush on me and how I didn't know what to do with that, because I didn't feel the same way about you. And the more earnest you were, the more I wanted to flee. Not from you, exactly. But from your feelings. They were strong and insistent, and I didn't know what to do with them.

And then you asked me to the Christmas dance and I said I wasn't going. And then another boy—one I did like—asked me to go and I said yes. That was a rotten thing to do. I realized it at the time, but I especially realized it when I saw you there that night. I don't think I'll ever forget the look on your face.

I've forgiven that sixteen year-old girl who stood up my son now, of course, although she didn't need my forgiveness. It's just that I finally saw myself in her and understood what made her do what she did.

Still. I wish I could take that moment at the Christmas dance back somehow.

Or at least let you know how sorry I am for how that felt to you.

YOUR TURN

Here's your chance to write that letter you've always been meaning to write. It could be a belated love letter, or a letter to clear up a misunderstanding. It could be an angry letter, where you finally say what you've wanted to say for a long time. See this exercise as an opportunity to share a little about your history and your values. The good news is you don't have to send it.

CHAPTER 18

Portraits

ANN'S TURN

My great-great grandmother, Patti Larsen.

I keep a framed black-and-white photo on my nightstand of my family having Christmas Eve dinner when I was four years old. All the usual suspects from my early childhood are there except for my mother who was taking the picture. The rest of them are there—my father, my grandfather, my grandmother holding my brother John, my great-uncle Bob and his wife Edna, whom we called Nanny, and my great-grandmother Pat sitting around a table set with my mother's best things.

Great-grandma Pat is white-haired and fairy-frail, her thin hands clasped together above the tablecloth like a small bird folding its wings. Looking at her in the photo, one might find it hard to believe that in her prime, she'd changed her name, kicked over the traces of her old life, left her Midwestern home, and landed in Ogden to work for the railroads. Along the way she acquired a husband and a son, shed the husband, and moved the son to Big Piney, Wyoming, where she eventually married the town banker and became the county's game warden. And the stories people told about her were epic in their scope.

Remember that time Patti stared down a bull?

Remember that time Patti drove a Model T around and around town until it finally stopped dead in its tracks, because she couldn't figure out how to turn it off?

Remember how she shouted at people to get out of her way while she was at it?

Remember how Patti always slept with a shotgun?

Remember how Patti always lied about her age on her fishing license until one day someone realized she'd officially become younger than her son?

As I've grown older, I've realized that some of the stories probably aren't technically true. But they are true to her spirit—or at least true to the way my mother remembers her grandmother.

They adored one another, those two. The truth is that my great-grandmother wasn't always there for her own son when he was growing up. But she more than made up for things with his daughter, my mother.

"Whenever we made a cake together," my mother remembers, "Grandma Pat would tell me to stir the batter slowly so we wouldn't make it dizzy." And then they'd pack up the cake, go fishing, have a fish fry, and eat the cake for dessert.

What did she look like when she was younger? I asked my mother.

She had auburn hair, my mother said. And she loved jewels the way a magpie loves things that shine.

Was she pretty? I wondered.

Yes. She was beautiful.

Later, when I saw pictures of my great-grandmother when she was a young woman, I was disappointed. From my mother's descriptions, I would have said she looked like Maureen O'Hara. But no. She was thin and tiny and truthfully rather ordinary-looking.

Except.

There was a liveliness about her expression in the photographs that was appealing—the kind of liveliness that could make people feel like they were in the presence of someone stunning.

And yes. Even in my Christmas photo of her—the one where she looks as fragile as angel hair—she dominates the scene. She's staring straight at the camera. Laughing.

LOUISE'S TURN

Portrait of My Father—a List

- He was breastfed until he was five. He can remember standing on the table and calling his mother when he was thirsty.
- He said he always wanted to work with electricity from the time he was young. He lived his dream.
- At 18, he began attending the Mormon Church in Utrecht because of a girl. He stood outside the building and counted down his jacket buttons: "I will go in. I won't go in. I will go in. I won't go in. I will go in." Did he know he had five buttons?
- He was engaged to someone else before my mother (that same girl). Then one day, he was sitting in church and noticed that she was holding his hand on one side and his best friend's hand on the other side. She married the best friend, but Daddy spoke at her funeral after she committed suicide in her sixties.
- I rode on the back of his bike in Holland.
- I rode in his old '38 Chevy in 1949. He liked driving up the canyons where the car vapor locked, and he went looking for water. I hated driving up the canyons. I preferred the bike, even though I once caught my foot in the spokes.
- He saved ten Dutch men from being taken to Nazi Germany by letting them out of the filled up concert hall where they were being held (and where he was the lighting technician). Most of the men were afraid to leave. Ten escaped. One of these men later stamped our passports before we boarded a ship.

- When *The New Amsterdam* came into New York harbor early one morning in late April, 1948, we stood on deck. My father lifted me up so that I could see the Statue of Liberty. Even writing it now makes me choke up.
- He entertained us by barking like a dog.
- When I was eight, he told the story of the Little Match Girl on Christmas Eve. I thought for years that he had made the story up himself. (He was a fine storyteller.) That was also the night my parents told me there was no Santa Claus. I was not surprised.
- He had an understated laugh: heh, heh, heh.
- He cheated at Checkers by playing "the Dutch rules," which made me yowl "Unfair!"
- He listened to the Salt Lake Bees baseball games on the radio the first year we were in America.
- Once he took some of us older kids bowling in downtown Salt Lake after midnight, because it was then half price. He bowled crooked. He showed us his crooked right arm. He broke it, he said, when he was about ten, and it didn't reset well. So, his mother took him back to the doctor, and the doctor, without warning, re-broke his arm over his knee and reset it.
- He saved part of a Twinkie from his lunch bucket to share with us.
- He let us ride the running board of his Thompson Electric truck down the alley when he came home from work.
- He had his appendix out when I was fifteen. Coming out of the anesthesia, he said, "Louise says I have a big nose, but I have a nose like Joseph Smith."
- Dinner wasn't a meal without potatoes.
- He loved *Perry Mason* the first one and ever after. He must have had them memorized.
- At dinner, he told us "Willy" stories. Willy was a young, new electrician he worked with.

- Later, he told us Mrs. Warshaw stories when they were working on Wasatch Towers, a co-op in Salt Lake City, where she was to live in the penthouse. Mrs. Warshaw had red hair.

- He took all the family pictures and later movies with his Super 8 camera.

- I don't know why he was referring to Henry III, but because of his Dutch accent, it came out "Henry the Turd." We fell down laughing.

- His favorite song in the fifties was "Oh My Papa," which he sang with a tortured exuberance at the top of his lungs.

- He taught me to drive a stick-shift in our blue, '51 Ford. He was not patient about it either, but hey, I learned.

- Whenever he returned to the Netherlands to visit his family, he was afraid he wouldn't be allowed to leave.

- He loved long baths.

- He whistled when he worked.

- Before digital, and after my father retired, he designed a switch box that would turn all the Christmas lights on at Temple Square at the same time. Before that, they relayed. The president of the Church at the time, Ezra Taft Benson, gave his Christmas devotional talk and was supposed to push a lever that would turned on all the lights. He forgot, and others on the stand, whispered loudly, "You forgot to turn on the lights!" Under his breath, President Benson said, "It doesn't work anyway." But, *Voila*, it did work. All the lights turned on with President Benson's bringing down the lever. Bravo, Louis Roos!

- He was devoted to the Mormon Church, where he served as a bishop (twice), stake president, patriarch, temple sealer. He and Mother served two missions, one in the Netherlands and one in the Bern, Switzerland temple. He was able to marry several of his grandchildren, which he did with humor and delightful storytelling.

- What he missed most after he joined the church: black tea (which the *Word of Wisdom*, a health code, doesn't allow).

Portrait of my Mother—a List

- She was the sixth child of ten.
- She played soccer as well as the boys.
- She could juggle three oranges.
- She wanted to go on to be a teacher, but her father couldn't afford to send her on for teacher training, so she became a domestic. (Only the brothers got trained for employment.)
- Once she rode her bike home smoking pastel, lady cigarettes
- She could beat anyone arm wrestling.
- She played softball.
- She was named after the first twin, who died: Geert.
- She fixed our bikes, sewed and knitted. She taught me how to knit when I was a Seagull in Primary. I refused to learn how to sew.
- When I was a teenager, she refereed for church girl's softball games.
- Dinner was on the table every night when my dad got home from work, except for Wednesdays, when she worked in Primary. That night we got Dee's Hamburgers.
- She belonged to the Book of the Month Club and subscribed to the Saturday Evening Post and the Lady's Home Journal. She was a reader and wrote better English than my father.
- She sang Dutch songs while she worked.
- She rode the bus downtown, and didn't learn how to drive a car until she was 54. It was she who washed the car on Saturdays.
- She made us practice our church talks until they were memorized.
- She laid out my father's clothes for him. She also bought his clothes.

- I once asked her if she told her mother things the way I told her, and she said, "Heavens, no!" She thought Americans were liars with their easy, fake compliments.
- She was the consummate manager.
- She did not suffer fools gladly.
- If she sent me to the store for a cabbage, I came home with a head of lettuce; if she sent me to the store for lettuce, I came home with a cabbage.
- She was moody.
- She made us nap in the summers and sent us to bed early, even when our friends were still playing outside.
- She kept treats for Daddy's lunch in her sock drawer.
- We began with an allowance of 25 cents. She paid us two dimes and five pennies so we could pay three cents tithing. We also got a dime for "a treat" that was not tithed.
- She used Veto deodorant and Halo shampoo.
- She kept to her household schedule: Monday washing, Tuesday ironing, etc.
- She talked to my aunts on the phone.
- She had rheumatic fever when I was ten and was supposed to stay in bed for three weeks, but on Fridays she got up and scrubbed the kitchen and bathroom floors on hands and knees and told me not to tell Daddy.
- She put function over beauty every time.
- In the fifties she lost a lot of weight with Dr. Waters, who basically sold amphetamines.
- She never learned to set her own hair, and preferred permanents.
- She could cut you down with "Puh."
- She washed the sidewalks on her knees in front of the house until she discovered the garden hose.
- She was shy and introverted.
- She had a great laugh.
- She hated calling on the phone and made my sister Janie do it for her. (I hate calling on the phone as well.)

- When life came to an impasse, she said, "Oh vel."
- I have no idea what she believed other than my father. Maybe that was enough.

YOUR TURN

A portrait is a verbal close-up of someone. Whether you describe that person in a narrative or in a list or as a dialogue, try to capture their essence with small details and mannerisms. Write about Mother, Father, grandparents, aunts, brothers, sisters, your best friend, a favorite teacher. You choose. And then choose again. Write fast. Write your first thoughts. Keep going.

CHAPTER 19

Holiday Celebrations

ANN'S TURN

Last February while we were working in the kitchen together, my son Geoffrey said, "Well, now I know why you love holidays so much. You get that from your mom."

We'd had dinner the night before at my mother's house, and even though none of us is in grade school anymore, she gave everybody a little valentine and some conversation hearts.

(By the way, I sometimes think about creating a line of conversation hearts that elementary school boys would find hilarious—hearts that say stuff like "I see London, I see France, I see our teacher's underpants." But it probably wouldn't fly and that's not the point anyway.)

The point is that my mother loves a holiday and she would no more let one slip by unobserved than she would let her beloved French poodle go without having his toenails painted.

She, my mother, inherited her love of holiday-making from her maternal grandmother, my rifle-toting great grandmother, Patti Larsen. (Not her real name. She changed it when she left her old life behind.) From what I hear, my Great-grandma Pat always went big on holidays—at least as big as possible in Big Piney, Wyoming, where water routinely froze in goldfish bowls on a winter's night. Her favorite was Christmas. According to my mother, she set a table with with linens and silver, china and crystals, then loaded it with roast turkey and yams, dressing, and mincemeat made out of deer she'd shot herself. Everyone was invited. Nieces. Nephews. Cousins. People who didn't have another place to be.

Not surprisingly, my mother's favorite holiday is Christmas. What I remember most clearly is the tree she trimmed for us, with its tinsel and glass balls that would distort your face like a funhouse mirror when you got close enough to see your reflection.

And I like Christmas, too, although as both a mother and a person who has worked holiday retail, I understand why people don't. When I asked my boys what they remember most about Christmas they said things like the food and the way they were allowed to open one present on Christmas Eve and the food and how our tree was the fattest, tallest tree on the block and also the food.

So yeah. We do Christmas in our family.

How do you celebrate Christmas—or any holiday in your family—and what does that say about you?

LOUISE'S TURN

On the whole my mother found American holidays fatuous and wasteful, especially Halloween. She would not let us go trick or treating after age 12. The same went for Easter baskets. After age 12, you were too old for all that nonsense. She never made any pretense that there was an Easter bunny or a tooth fairy, although we did get money for lost teeth. She, of course, allowed us to buy Valentine cards for school and we had the crepe paper and colored paper necessary to make a Valentine's box, but other than that she remained aloof. My mother did not give parties of any kind, including birthday parties with outsiders. She had had china and silver in Holland, but sold it before immigrating. Later, she bought a set of dishes and flatware for entertaining, but that was long after I was married.

We did have birthday celebrations at home, and she was especially good at buying lavish cakes, which I enjoyed. She never baked anything but bread. Baked goods were bought at Dunford's Bakery on Ninth East. For a long while she bought the most fabulously decorated birthday cakes from a Dutch baker. We sang, blew out candles and received presents.

When I was ten, I was obsessed with having a birthday party with all my friends, but she said no. I kept hoping for a "surprise party," but the day passed without any surprises. I realize now, that my mother would have been nonplussed as to how to put an American birthday party together. I was asking for the impossible, and I knew never to ask again.

Both parents liked Christmas. We asked for what we wanted. We knew not to be outrageous about our requests. Mother kept a small black book in the top drawer of her desk in her bedroom where she listed each child's name and exactly every item they were getting. I always knew what I was getting.

The gifts were hidden in a closet behind the swinging door that led from the dining room into the hallway to the kitchen. This door remained shut with a hook most of the time, and we didn't think of looking there until I was in 4th grade. And one Saturday, we children got behind that door and looked at *everything*. And we learned that it wasn't very fun to have seen your Christmas presents in advance, and that it made us feel smarmy, and we never did it again.

We helped decorate the tree, and when we went to bed, Mother redid the whole thing. We especially liked the candles that bubbled. I'm guessing my father bought these.

We children never slept on Christmas Eve, but sang carols all night long and then at 5 a.m. began sending the youngest and most charming child into our parents' room to ask if we could get up. Often we could. We'd run into the dining room en mass, hollering and hyperventilating. My father would yell, "Stop!" And we stood shivering in the doorway while he took a snapshot of the tree with the presents. Then we were onto the gifts like vultures at a coyote feast. My parents sat in their pajamas watching and smiling. We opened everything as the room filled with cast-off wrapping paper. We'd play and eat candy from our stockings and slowly everyone carried their stuff off to their bedrooms for display and maybe even take a nap. We dressed in new clothes and visited our friends and they visited us. The afternoon included a big dinner and playing new board games (which were always given to my sister, Janie, because she took good care of the various parts). Mother often played with us. The best part about living in a large family was that when you got bored with your own toys, you could move on to your little brother's Lincoln Logs. Daddy often liked to hide nuts and candies in the late afternoon and he would tell us if we were "hot or cold" as we hunted about. I remember Christmas fondly, with both parents fully present and engaged.

YOUR TURN

We, Ann and Louise, write about holidays differently. This should give you permission (if you still need permission) to write honestly about your own holiday traditions. Were your people party animals, or more restrained with holidays? Or were they manipulative: "You're not getting anything for Christmas unless you shape up!" Or did they forget holidays altogether? It happens. Write about what *was*, not the way you wish it had been. Striving for authenticity should be one of the memoirist's foremost goals.

CHAPTER 20

What Are Your Beliefs?

LOUISE'S TURN

I believe in God, but He is not easy. His silence overwhelms me, and yet I am one of those people who can say what she wants aloud to the universe, and it happens. Who do I thank, if not God? I have no idea about Him, except that he's bigger than the night sky. I sense him most in music, literature and art. I sense him in cultivated fields and flower gardens, and whenever I am in a small boat on a placid sea.

I believe in Jesus and the atonement. I don't know the how of it. I like Jesus in the scriptures: the commitment to the spirit of the law rather than the letter of the law. I like his discussions on love rather than judgment, on caring for the poor. I like the Jesus, who challenges hypocrisy, and overturns the tables of the moneychangers in the temple. I like the Jesus who likes women. I like the reclusive and private Jesus who tries to escape the crowds by getting in a boat, or climbing a mountain, or setting off for forty days and forty nights.

I like the Jesus, who says, "Fear not, little flock." Mostly, I like the Jesus who heals despite our unbelief.

I believe in perpetual responsibility but not in unconditional love.

I believe we should see the world through a kind eye and give others the benefit of the doubt.

I believe in a hereafter, because I find it impossible not to believe.
I believe the glass is half empty.
I believe wearing tap shoes can change your life.
I believe we should not take offense. The world is what it is.
I believe religion should not be a competitive sport.
I believe other people's stories about seeing dead loved ones, but I don't see them myself and don't expect to.

Although, when Sharon Kamarath was dying, she said she wanted a way to show us all that she was still a living being after she died. She decided to return as a button(s) (she was a seamstress). Her husband, David, was finding buttons around her gravesite before all the mourners left. All of her family members have found peculiar buttons in odd places.

Colleen saw a black and brown plaid button on the floor of Deseret Industries, but dismissed it being a "Sharon sighting," because the D.I. is filled with old clothes and loose buttons. When she returned to her car, she found the identical black and brown plaid button on her baby's car seat. That's a Sharon sighting.

I was in on a button sighting with Sharon's daughter, Sarah, who is my daughter-in-law, and my son, Sam, and Nancy Davies, the real estate agent, when we were looking at an open house in Bountiful, Utah. All four of us entered the house at the front and inspected the wood floors in the living room. In fact, we questioned whether it was a wood floor or an engineered floor, so we examined it carefully.

Then we moved through the rest of the house. When we returned to the living room, there was a white-shirt-button on the living room floor. It had not been there the first time we went through, and there was no one else in the house. We accused each other of placing the button there. None of us was missing buttons, nor did the found button match our own buttons.

I believe in Sharon Kamarath, who believed in God, Jesus, and a hereafter, and who has been spreading buttons in the most unlikely places. I can hear her say, "So, now what do you think, Louise?"

I believe Fred Astaire made more people happy than Moses.

I believe things will always get worse. Thank heaven for *Masterpiece Theater* and Netflix.

I believe in smiling at strangers everywhere (not grinning, which makes you look stupid).

I believe in giving large tips. Waiters get paid next to nothing.

I believe all men look handsome in a classic tuxedo.

I believe you should always have your passport up to date in case someone wants to take you to Paris, France in a giddy moment.

I believe most women could use a little make-up.

I believe humor is the gift that keeps on giving.

I believe you can't own too many red jackets.

I believe even God loves a well-designed, fast car.

I believe beauty is more important than truth or goodness.

I believe even people in first-world countries should be allowed to whine five minutes a year.

I believe that grandchildren are the most surprising benefit of old age.

ANN'S TURN

I believe that depressed people should own a dog.

I believe that everybody should plant at least one tomato plant every spring, even if they never succeed in getting tomatoes. It's a hopeful thing to do.

I believe that kindness is a more admirable trait than intelligence.

And speaking of intelligence, I believe it comes in all shapes and sizes.

I believe that status and rank are overrated and that whenever possible, we should politely ignore them.

I believe you can tell a lot about a person by the way he treats the people who can't do anything for him.

I believe that exercise is good for the body and even better for the soul.

I believe that having low expectations actually increases your level of happiness in this life.

I believe that football as we know it will no longer exist fifty years from now.

I believe that would make me sad—if I were still around to watch a game.

I believe in having a pile of books by my bedside at all times, even if I never get around to reading them all.

I believe that there are no easy solutions to the country's big problems. Same goes for the world's problems, and anybody who tells you differently has a crate of snake oil in the trunk of his car to sell you.

I believe the good things about people can also be the challenging things about them.

I believe a woman should be able to do whatever she wants with her hair.

I believe a person should spend as much time outside as possible.

I believe an individual should not be denied opportunity based on gender or race.

I believe that compromise is not a dirty word.

I believe that there is more than one way to skin a cat.

Not that I believe in skinning cats.

I believe that no matter how old you get, you need people in your life who remember the same music, the same movies, the same current events that you do. You need your peers.

I believe children should be given space without constant adult direction.

I believe money spent on a good meal in a restaurant is never money wasted.

I believe, if possible, you should find a way to keep talking to your siblings.

I believe that associating only with people who see the world the same way you do leads to myopia.

I believe that travel—even if you don't travel far from home—creates its own kind of literacy.

Where politicians are concerned I definietly believe in an aggressive press.

I believe all people are hypocrites in one way or another, so we should all cut each other a little slack.

I believe people should discover what they're good at doing and then do it.

I believe it's stupid to take offense. Most people don't mean to offend, and even if they do, why give them power over you?

I believe that the experience of failing is often more valuable than the experience of succeeding.

I believe that things could be worse and they probably will be, so why not find something about your present situation to enjoy?

I believe you should take care of your family and remain loyal to your friends.

And finally, I believe that shoes should be comfortable and pants should be stretchy.

YOUR TURN

Plenty of writers have observed that they don't know what they think until they write it down. The same might hold true for beliefs. We may not know what we really believe until we set those beliefs down on paper. Of all the exercises in this book, this one is the most rewarding. Enlist friends and family members to write down their beliefs too.

CHAPTER 21

Creating a Persona

ANN'S TURN

Read the following section from a personal essay and then describe the person who wrote it:

There it was, nearly 500 degrees in the shade, and I was playing tennis in the middle of a summer afternoon with my seven-year-old son, Alec, because I was trying to be a Good Mother.

"Okay! Your serve," I called to him gamely.

Alec promptly lobbed his ball into the center of the net.

"Fifteen-Love," he screamed. "I'm totally wasting you, Mom!"

"Um. Wait a minute, Sweetheart," I said. "The ball didn't go over the net. Technically speaking, it's my point."

Alec snorted. "Yeah, right."

So that's how things went with us. Alec kept hitting the ball into the net and giving himself points for it, and in the end I lost. Big time.

"Geez," Alec said as we crawled into our car to leave. "You pretty much stink at tennis, Mom."

How would you describe the narrator here? Overwhelmed? Ironic? Slightly depressed but funny? Game for new experiences but mildly suspicious about where it's all going? Cranky in a good-natured sort of way?

In this chapter Louise and I will discuss persona. What is persona you ask? For our purposes, we'll define it as the individual you present yourself as being to your reader.

Hold on. Waaiiit a minute, you say. Shouldn't we just be ourselves when we write? Especially if we are writing our life stories?

Of course. But there's a whole lotta you, right? It's taken your family and friends—and especially yourself—an entire lifetime to (sort of) figure you out. Your reader, on the other hand, doesn't have an entire lifetime to do the same thing. Your reader needs you to be a narrator they can readily get a handle on. In fact, they need to experience you as a character (Sherlock Holmes! Scarlett O'Hara! Harry Potter! Winnie the Pooh!) who has a story to tell.

This doesn't mean you have to be locked into one kind of story. Some of your stories can be happy. Others can be sad. Or angry. Or grumpy. Or... But stories told by a well-defined narrator with specific tastes and identifiable characteristics go a long way to capturing and keeping a reader's interest. And readers do enjoy the feeling of listening to or reading stories by someone they know.

Now back to that paragraph you read earlier. The author was none other than myself, writing about the soul-crushing experience of playing tennis with a young, overly confident male.

I often appear in my essays as a slightly bemused observer of life. And that's because I am a slightly bemused observer of life. Why do people—myself included—do the crazy things they do? This bemused observer is who I am when I write— but it's not all of me.

The rest of me gets to be a little bit private.

And that's just fine with me.

LOUISE'S TURN

Discussing persona is a little like advising a teenager to be herself when she's about to go on her first date. Which self?

A writing persona is a public personality that is so close to the real you, that readers sometimes think it is you. For example, I've had readers say that it would be so fun to live with me, because I'd make them laugh all day.

No, I say, you wouldn't like it. I'm a depressive. They shake their heads in disbelief. Who they really want to live with is my persona. So would I.

Persona is the edited self. It is a consistent voice readers recognize. The persona can be humorous, elegant or loutish, but it is a choice the writer makes. Persona is entertainment. It is also a boundary between the writer's real life and what she chooses to present as her real life. The writer watches Netflix while eating pickled herring in bed and forgets to changer her underwear. The persona transforms her questionable behavior to something charming and humorous.

There's a difference between infusing your imperfect life with humor and/or drama, and just plain lying your face off. I can write about my anxiety when I first went to Paris, but I mustn't write about going to Paris when I didn't actually go. Or, for that matter, write about anxiety if I don't actually have anxiety. If I wanted to do that, I should call it fiction, because that's what it is. Out and out lying about your own life in a memoir may come back and bite you in the butt.

And finally, you don't have to spill all of your guts onto the page. Ann and I may sound like we have no boundaries, because we have a high threshold for humiliating ourselves publicly, but believe me when I say, what we don't tell you about our lives would fill volumes.

You make the decision about your own presentation. That's persona.

YOUR TURN

Try this exercise designed to help you understand the concept of "persona."

First, think about an embarrassing experience you've had. The more embarrassing the better. Write a paragraph about this experience using the following personas:

- Try writing about it as if you're fourteen and chewing gum.
- Write it again sounding like your mother or grandmother.

- Write about it so you sound like Snoop Dog or the rapper of your choice.
- Then write it sounding like yourself.

What we hope is that this exercise will help you understand that persona is created by the words you select, as well as the attitude you take toward your experience.

Don't think of persona as a mask. You're not hiding. You are choosing the public part of your authentic self that shares your life stories.

CHAPTER 22

Writing Dialogue

LOUISE'S TURN

Some people deserve to be broadly heard, and hiding them behind indirect discourse just doesn't work. They need their own voice. You can give it to them by writing dialogue.

Undoubtedly, you will want to point out that you cannot remember conversations exactly; you only remember the gist of what was said. What to do?

Remembering the gist is enough. The rest is filled in with your imagination. You know what was said. You know the intent. You know the result. Fill in the gaps with your imagination. Take it seriously. I had to do it with the piece below where my father convinces me that hot dogs are made from dog tails. I was fifteen! How did he get me to cave?

The way he played checkers gave me a clue. When he was kinged, he would move the king across the board diagonally in one sweeping motion taking out any of my pieces that happened to be in the way.

"You can't do that!" I was appalled. "That's cheating!"

"No it's not." He swept his king in the other direction, cleaning up the board.

"That's not in the rules!"

"It's in the Dutch rules."

"We're not playing Dutch rules. I've never heard of any Dutch rules."

"I always play the Dutch rules," my father said. He turns to my mother. "I won," he said.

My mother pursed her lips into the tiniest of smiles. She loved Dutch cheaters.

Having played checkers with my father helped me imagine how he might have gotten me to believe that hot dogs are made from dog tails. Certainly he would have gone "Dutch."

This conversation happened at dinnertime. I sat at the opposite end of the kitchen table from my father. Possibly we were eating fried hotdogs, one of Mother's staples.

"You know hot dogs are made from dog tails," my father began with his thesis.

I am deeply skeptical. "Oh sure." I rolled my eyes.

"It's true," he said.

"Stupid." I said. What I wanted to say was *you can be so stupid*.

"That's why so many people won't eat hotdogs, because they think it's a trashy meat," he said. "They're spiced up so you can't actually tell what you're eating."

I liked that spicy goodness. "They're not dog tails," I said.

"You see those short-haired dogs with the stubby tails? The vet trims them and they use the cut-off part as hotdogs. Just the right size." He keeps eating his dinner. "They have a special machine that removes the hair."

"Daddy!"

"It's true. In Holland they had to mark 'dog tail' on the packaged hotdogs, but they don't do that in America."

It was then that I remembered him telling me that during the war, people tried to sell skinned cats as rabbit meat, but later, the rabbit heads were left on the body, so that customers knew they were buying rabbit and not a cat for supper.

"We ate plenty of hotdogs in Holland. Didn't we, Mother?" He glanced at my mother, who as the straight man, stared at her plate.

"We didn't care if they were 'Kooikerhondjes.'"

That detail sounded convincing. Even though I didn't know exactly what a Kooikerhondje was, I knew that hondje was a dog.

"Kooikerhondjes." It curled my tongue.

"That's dog tails in Dutch."

"Yeah? Is that true?"

"Cross my heart," which he does.

"Gee."

He looks at me, a smile starting at the corners of his mouth turning to a laugh: "heh, heh, heh." He elbows my mother. "I got her that time."

I have to say that this began as a rush write, but when I realized I was going to have to come up with a Dutch word, I had to stop and Google Dutch dogs. I chose this particular word, because it ended in "hondje," a word I would have recognized. A Kooikerhondje is a breed of dog, not a hot dog.

It is true, though, that during the extreme conditions of Nazi occupied Holland, people did try to sell off cats as rabbits. Like any good liar, my father made good use of half-truths.

ANN'S TURN

I love Louise's perspective on this essay: if you know the gist of a conversation, you can bring that conversation back to life (like Frankenstein!) by using dialogue that has been invented to some extent.

This, of course, is a luxury I do not have when I'm wearing my Journalist Hat. Whenever I quote people in the newspaper, everyone expects me to be *completely* accurate—the person interviewed, my editor, and our readers. That's as it should be.

But memoir presumes a different kind of accuracy. And sometimes the truest picture of what happened is captured by dialogue you have distilled from the moments you remember.

Go for it!

And watch me put on my Memoirist Hat and go for it myself as I recall the ongoing good-natured argument my father and I used to have about Hank Williams' music when I was in high school. Our conversations went something like this.

DAD: You wanna listen to a little Hank Williams right now?
ME: No. Not now. Not ever.
DAD: Why?
ME: Because it's redneck music.
DAD: What?
ME: You heard what I said. I'm a doper. Not a roper. (And okay. I'm not really a doper, either).
DAD: Well, let me tell you what. Hank Williams' music is the music of the people.
ME: Which people? Not my people!
DAD: Come on. Hank sings about all the stuff that matters. Life. Love. Loss. Trains and honky-tonkin'.
ME: UGH! PLEASE! STOP!
DAD: Mark my words. One day you'll love Hank.
ME: Never.

What's the moral of this re-imagined conversation? That you should never say "never." Especially when you're a teenager. Because here's the deal. One summer evening you'll be driving your car with the windows down and you'll hear Hank's voice—clear as the night sky—come over the radio, and then you'll recall the lyrics to "I'm So Lonesome I Could Cry," and before you know it, you'll be crying, too.

Do you know why?

Because my dad was right. Hank sings about the stuff that matters.

And sometimes you just have to grow up a little to know that.

YOUR TURN

Write a strand of remembered dialogue between two people: you could recreate a conversation you had with someone else, or a conversation you overheard.

Don't get all fancy with dialogue tags. Use "he said," and "she said," instead of "he growled," or "she snapped." Unless, "he" is a tiger and "she" is a turtle.

Also, avoid adverbs that tell us *how* something was said: "she said, *dreamily*," or "he said, *sadly*." Let the dialogue and context speak for themselves.

CHAPTER 23

Establishing Boundaries

ANN'S TURN

So we have this story in my family . . .

When my brother, John and I were little, our mother decided it was time to teach us some table manners. So she bought a china piggy bank and explained that whenever we did something inappropriate—talked with our mouths full, reached for food instead of asking someone to please pass it, or put our elbows on the table— she would put "the china pig" in front of our plate. This was supposed to shame us into behaving like well-mannered children instead of pigs. *China* pigs.

Here's what happened. As soon as I saw that fake pig sitting in the middle of the table at Sunday dinner, I couldn't help myself: I oinked. And then I oinked again. After which I collapsed into hysterical giggles.

This reaction is *not* what my mother had in mind. Furious, she snatched the pig away and we never saw it again.

Great story, right? Only when John tells it, he says *he* was the one who oinked. And then oinked again. After which *he* collapsed into hysterical giggles.

What's my point? It's this: memory is a slippery customer. Family members may (and regularly do) remember the same events differently. That's why when anybody in your family says, "But that is not how it happened," you should immediately say, "Then you write your *own* version."

In fact, if you're in the mood for a little family activity, pass around paper and pens and ask everyone to write down what they remember about an iconic family story—the time your sister got locked out of the house in her underwear, or your brother shoplifted a pack of cigarettes in front of a plain clothes police officer, or your mother delivered a child in the car, because your father had to finish watching the end of the Super Bowl. You might be surprised (and interested) in various versions of the same tale.

Other issues arise when writing about our nearest and dearest. Boundaries, for instance. The truth is that individuals have different levels of comfort with sharing personal information. I have one son, for instance, who's made the decision not to post any photos of his children online. Another son posts thousands of photos of his child on a daily basis. So what are memoir writers to do if they have both types of people in their lives?

My rule of thumb is to know what *your* values and boundaries are, and let yourself be guided by those, even if other people don't always like what you write. Here are two of my values:

1. Honesty. Personally, I'm not a devotee of lifestyle tastemakers who always present themselves—their homes, their families, their gardens, their pets—in a positive light. Look at this! I've got it made! And if you follow my recipes or instructions or whatever, you'll be as awesome as I am. It's soooo easy! Yes, I like to see the positive and the pretty, but I also like to see rough edges and the real costs of living authentic lives.

2. Kindness. Usually. I come from a family who laughs a lot— and laughs at themselves and each other a lot. This has turned out to be a pretty healthy way for us to live. So yeah, I poke fun at things—usually myself. But I hope I do it in a way that never feels overly mean, or in a way that feels like I'm just trying to settle a grudge.

I will say this. My family had its share of typical family drama, but it was basically a functional, intact family. I have many friends whose childhoods were dark, presided over by the troubles of extremely troubled adults. I think they should feel free to write about those times and those people honestly. A lot of damage is done to families and the communities we reside in by keeping things shrouded by secrets.

And now for a word about my boundaries.

I'm comfortable with writing about a lot of stuff that other people wouldn't be. I've written about how our family spent one summer in bed, because we all had hepatitis, which is one of those low-rent diseases that people don't like to acknowledge. I've written about mental illness and losing babies. I've written about the fact that I struggle with my weight, and that I'm a lousy housekeeper.

But there are some things I won't write about. In-laws, for example. Honey, that is just a can of worms best left on the food storage shelf. And even though I'm not a prude, I don't like to write much about sex.

Oh, wait a minute.

I *am* a prude.

The point is that you can and should set your own boundaries.

LOUISE'S TURN

Never change the names of the guilty. I first heard that phrase in graduate school, and I've repeated it to my own students, who snicker like I did when I first heard it. I think we snickered, because we could. We had no history of continual brutality or practiced meanness in our lives, no characters we felt needed protection from their own shameful behavior, or from their own names. Now that I am old, I'm okay with changing the names of the guilty if it's possible.

It may not be possible. If you were sexually abused through your childhood by Mom or Dad, or your only brother, then there will always be people, close relatives and friends, who know exactly who you're writing about. Even without using her given name, Mom is always Mom. Dad is always Dad. Whether you like it or not, these people, who were supposed to protect and love you, but didn't, are part of your growing up and need to be included in your life's story. Abuse in childhood has shaped the adult you have become. Tell it as a survivor.

Balance out the grizzly with what was good in your life at the time. A friend? A pet? A tree to sit in? A kind neighbor or coach? Dancing, playing football, singing in a chorus? What made the unbearable, bearable? Where did you find small pockets of safety? If there is a redemption story in there—"after they took a tumor the size of a grapefruit out of my father's head, he became a completely different person," or "after my mother found Jesus, she became more loving"—then go ahead and tell it. Most stories of abuse don't come with a clean redemption for the wrong doer. Don't make one up.

It isn't just victims of abuse who find it hard to tell their tale. Almost every beginning writer has the thought that all relatives and acquaintances must be dead before they can tell their own story. If the only thing holding you back from writing about your life is a few names of boyfriends, girlfriends and teachers, then by all means, change the names. Change everyone's name, but remember, Mom is always Mom and Dad is always Dad.

They weren't perfect, were they? Even if they didn't say it out loud, the body language, the looks, the tones of their voices, the silences said it for them: you're boring, you're inadequate, you're a coward, you're disappointing, you're lazy, you're clumsy, you're stupid, you look terrible, you're sickly, you're weird, you make me tired, you act like your father's side of the family, and they were all crazy—I could go on and on. In fact, I have.

To write about growing up in families is to write about our humanity. Tell the truth, but write with compassion and humor.

The only time my father hit me was when I was praying. It's true. He came into the back bedroom to listen to my nightly prayers. To keep him there as long as possible, I listed everyone and everything I was thankful for. It was a long, very long, manipulative list. He saw that it would never end, and swiped me in the side of the head.

I said, "Amen." He tucked me in and left.

It was a good lesson for a future writer: always be aware of your audience.

YOUR TURN

Helpful Hint! If you want to tell a true story but know that some people in your life won't appreciate being "outed," go ahead and change their names. Or withhold their names. As Ann's boys got older and resented the attention they received, because their crazed columnist mother blabbed about them in the newspaper, she started referring to them generically as "my sons." This (mostly) worked as a compromise.

Helpful Hint Redux! If you're truly worried about how someone will react, think about getting permission. And then you can honor their wishes. Or not. Ann once asked her dad if she could write about that time when, as a young man he felt like beating up a bishop at a church ballgame. He said no. She's honored that request for many years. Until now.

CHAPTER 24

Alternative Lives

LOUISE'S TURN

Who hasn't dreamed of alternative lives? Maybe in some parallel universe someone exactly like me is living my alternative lives. I'd like to have a peek at that. Anyway, here goes:

Alternative life #1: My parents don't immigrate to America in 1948, and I grow up in Utrecht, the Netherlands. I go to art school and become an artist of mixed talent and later become a writer—a writer in Dutch. I try to translate my novels into English, hoping for a wider audience, but because I wasn't paying attention in school, my verb tenses are all haywire. No matter, because I live in a 17th century apartment across from the Vondelpark in Amsterdam.

Alternative life #2: I decide never to marry and fly to NYC the day after high school graduation. On the plane, I change my name to Louisa Rose and walk up to first class where there is an empty seat for me. I get a job at Mademoiselle magazine and work my way up to Editor of Big and Important Things while going to night school at City College. At forty, I have a nervous breakdown, because my life is materialistic and hollow. I fly to an ashram in India, where I write a bestselling book, *EAT, PRAY, LOVE.*

Oh wait! That's someone else's life. Sorry.

Alternative life #3: Tom and I decide quite rationally that we don't want children, and live out our lives in complete peace and harmony in Vienna, Austria where we live in a large apartment inside the Ring and never buy groceries anywhere but the Julius Meinl am Graben. We, of course, dispense smug advice on childrearing and budgeting your time and money to all of our friends, who struggle like worms in a can to survive. Then we get new friends.

Alternative life #4: While I am on vacation in NYC, I witness a crime in which a Mafia boss, using a garish tie, strangles a man in an elevator at the Excelsior Hotel on the Upper West Side. I testify in court and then am whisked away into the Witness Protection Program under the name Annie Roosevelt. Preferably in Paris, France.

Poor Tom is left with four sons and a huge mortgage.

Alternative life #5: I become a character actress and win an Oscar for playing Meryl Streep's mother. Meryl Streep wins her fourth Oscar for playing my daughter. She and I become BFFs.

Alternative life #6: Tom and I retire to a restored school house on Prince Edward Island and raise black and white chickens (Plymouth Rocks), because I think they look pretty on the green lawn leading to the Gulf of St. Laurence. Soon, I realize that chickens poop, and someone has to clean it up. Tom is too old and tired to do it. All of Prince Edward Island now smells of chicken poop. It ruins this alternative life, so I return to Alternative Life #2 where I never marry (see above).

ANN'S TURN

Instead of alternative lives, this assignment puts me in mind of previous lives.

I only say this because I once went to a psychic who (after closing her eyes and giving it a good think) told me I have always been exactly who I am now. I've wondered what she meant by this and now I think I know.

PRE-HISTORIC ME: I live somewhere in central France with my husband and our three (surviving) children. My husband paints cave walls for a living. He's mostly happy in his job, but sometimes he complains. "Bison, bison, bison. That's all people want me to paint these days. What I wouldn't give to paint a horse now and then." Meanwhile I have misplaced my club again. "Has anybody seen my club?" I ask.

MEDIEVAL ME: I live in a nunnery in Flanders, where I spend my days doing embroidery and praying—that is when I can find my rosary. "Has anybody seen my rosary?" I ask.

POLYNESIAN ME: I live in Hawaii shortly before Captain Cook shows up and ruins all the reindeer games for my people and me. This is my favorite lifetime by far, because, you know. Sea! Sand! Sun! Too bad I can't remember where I parked my canoe. "Has anybody seen my canoe?" I ask.

REVOLUTIONARY ME: Somehow I wind up in America, fighting against the British who want to tax my tea because you know how the British are—always taxing tea whenever they get the chance. It's a dodgy, dangerous life, mostly because I can't find my musket. "Has anybody seen my musket?" I ask.

NEW YORK ME: It's the 1950's. I'm in a gang called the Sharks. My gang likes to wear tight pants and have dance-offs with a rival gang called the Jets. The only problem is that I can't always find my tight pants. "Has anybody seen my tight pants?" I ask.

ME ME: The year is 2015. I meet twice a week in a downtown library with my friend Louise Plummer where we write this book. Sometimes I'm late, though, because I can't find my keys.

"Has anybody seen my keys?" I ask.

YOUR TURN

Why not have some fun about writing about your fake lives? Just resist the temptation to publish it as an actual piece of memoir; otherwise you might get chewed out by Oprah in front of millions of people on TV.

CHAPTER 25

Obituary

ANN'S TURN

We're coming to the end. You will be one day too. Write your own obituary. No one knows better what was important enough for you to include in an obituary. It's an agonizing thing for relatives to do after you've gone. Write it yourself. Remember every word costs money. Here's mine:

Ann Cannon was fond of saying that the last thing out of her mouth on this earth would be a swear word.

She was right. It was.

Whenever Ann taught creative writing classes, she told her students that a fictional character could be defined by his or her likes and dislikes. And so in honor of her memory, we offer this glimpse into the things that Ann loved, along with a few of the things she didn't.

For starters, she hated the new parking meters in downtown Salt Lake City. They were Moriarty to her Sherlock Holmes. Unbeknownst to her one afternoon, her old friend and colleague, the Salt Lake Tribune columnist Robert Kirby, sat across the street and watched her deal with one of the kiosks. Kicking and cursing, he reported later, were involved.

She also disliked sitting through lectures and meetings, which made going to school and church a challenge for her. She struggled with a certain kind of nervous energy—a totally useless commodity for actually getting anything real done—throughout most of her life.

What else did she dislike? Piety. Pretentiousness. The rain. Feeling trapped. In any way. Ann would park on the street (in spite of the meters) a mile away from her destination before availing herself of nearby underground parking. She also always insisted on taking her own car places so that she could flee at a moment's notice, although she rarely did. Fortunately, she married a man who gave her a lot of space.

Speaking of which, Ann and Ken Cannon were married most of their lives to one another. While they certainly had their differences, they enjoyed each other's company. Ken had the extremely attractive habit of laughing at all of Ann's jokes. She appreciated that. Meanwhile, she loved his intelligence and his loyalty and the way he always shouted at the TV whenever he disagreed with what was being said on "Meet the Press."

What else did she love? Her kids. Their families. Her parents. Her brothers and their families. Friends. Flower gardens. Garden gnomes. Most any kind of music, but especially bluegrass and rock n' roll. Hiking. Traveling. Dancing. Knitting socks. Lying on the beach and listening to the ocean. Dogs. All of them. Cats, too. Baseball. Football. Cold cans of Dr. Pepper. Tomatoes warmed by the sun. Mexican food. A good mystery. Picture books. Awesome trivia. Summer. The sky at night.

There was sadness in Ann's life. A lot of it sometimes. But all in all, she had a good run.

LOUISE'S TURN

It was Ann who got me to write my obituary when she asked several Utah writers to write their own obituaries for her newspaper column. Mine is tongue in cheek. I'll probably have to write another one, but maybe not:

After a courageous battle with female patterned balding, complicated with sagging earlobes, author Louise Plummer finally dropped into that dark, humiliating, abyss for good. She was 72.

Her four loving sons texted each other as she expired. One of them was heard to say, "She's dead? I missed it."

It was her husband, Tom, of fifty years, who recorded her last words: "I hope I'm wearing lip gloss."

All who knew her will remember her for her scatological humor, her use of profanity in front of the grandchildren, and her manic guffaws.

Plummer taught English for twenty-two years, but was still conflicted about the Oxford comma at the time of her death.

Utah authors commenting on her death: "Who?" "Oh yes, a midlist novelist." "I thought she died years ago."

To save money, the family will skype her funeral from the study, a room she seldom used. If you miss it, go to YouTube. "Louise Plummer, no average Joe."

In lieu of flowers—whaat? There is no *in lieu of flowers*. Send flowers. Boatloads of them. Not plants. Cut flowers. Send cut flowers. Out of your garden, if you like. Send flowers. She wouldn't want anything else.

YOUR TURN

What are obituaries if not mini-memoirs? Take a moment to distill the essential facts of your life into an obituary. And for a fabulously informative and witty look at the art of obituary writing, check out *The Dead Beat: Lost Souls, Lucky Stiffs, and the Perverse Pleasures of Obituaries* by Marilyn Johnson.

AFTERWORD

So here we are at the end.

Except this ending is actually a beginning. For you. It's a time for you to begin *your* memoir, time for you to tell *your* stories. Seriously. You can do it. Here are some reminders:

1. Think in terms of memoir rather than autobiography. A memoir is more focused than autobiography. Memoir covers certain periods of your life as opposed to your entire life. *Don't Let's Go to the Dogs Tonight* by Alexandra Fuller, for example, focuses on her chaotic Rhodesian childhood, while *Leaving Before the Rains Come* by the same author deals with her divorce. Memoir can also be used to touch on certain recurring "themes" in your life.

2. Don't let fear stop you from writing your story. Sometimes we're afraid of offending or hurting people in our lives. Mostly we're afraid of not being good enough to write our stories. Just remember this: they're your stories. You should be the one to write them.

3. Set goals for yourself. Ann says: When I really want to get to work, I give myself a modest word count to hit Monday through Friday. When I'm having trouble getting started, I shoot for 500, which is only two pages. Sometimes I even shoot for 250 words. If you're consistent, you can write a memoir, a book in no time at all.

4. You don't need to know where your memoir is going when you first start writing. You may begin writing with a certain idea in mind, only to discover something else

more compelling along the way. But you won't have that experience unless you start writing. Meanwhile, you will eventually discover your memoir's "shape"—the way you choose to tell your story. This is a lovely opportunity for you to learn to trust the process.

5. Look at the models we've provided. Play around and see what triggers your memories. Give yourself time and permission to do a lot of "free writing." Again, you'll begin to notice certain recurring themes—your relationship with your father, for example—which may eventually suggest ways for you to structure your narrative.

6. Remember to use specific details that engage your readers' senses—how the sun felt on your bare arms when you rode your bike, how your grandmother's house always smelled like lavender and furniture polish, how the sound of crickets lulled you to sleep at night. Also focus on those telling details that say so much about the people in your life. When former president Bill Clinton introduced his wife, Hillary, at the DNC in 2016, he humanized her by mentioning how she lined their daughter's dorm room drawers with paper when they helped her move in.

7. Finally, feel joy in the process. Sometimes remembering can be painful. Writing can be painful. That's why it's useful to remind yourself of your good fortune. You have stories. You have the opportunity to tell them. What could be more hopeful?

You can do it!
You're not boring after all!

Made in the USA
Middletown, DE
22 January 2020